CLIPPINGS FROM THE PAST

Newspaper Stories of the East Riding of Yorkshire from a hundred years ago

Compiled by
David Bowman

HUTTON PRESS
1990

Published by the Hutton Press Ltd.,
130 Canada Drive, Cherry Burton,
Beverley, North Humberside HU17 7SB.

Phototypeset and printed by Image Colourprint Ltd.,
Anlaby, Hull.

ISBN 1 872167 10 1

CONTENTS

Page

Front Cover – Top: Market Weighton
Bottom: Bishop Wilton

INTRODUCTION

My reason for writing this book is quite simple. Whilst researching into the history of the mill buildings belonging to R. M. English Ltd., Pocklington, I discovered that in 1896 a huge fire had gutted that building.

Reading on through the newspapers I discovered that in 1897, after having been rebuilt, it was opened as the VICTORIA HALL – a purpose built concert/community hall. I have reproduced in this book that fire, the opening of the Victoria Hall and, because of the fire, the formation of the Pocklington Fire Brigade.

It became immediately obvious to me that there was sufficient interesting and newsworthy stories to fill a book, from that period a century ago.

What I have attempted to do is to reproduce stories from all over the East Riding. Hopefully all aspects of late Victorian life have been covered – from land, sea and air – from rural and urban centres of the county.

For me, on completion of the manuscript, I am thankful not to have lived during the 1890's. If you were wealthy, fine, these were "Good old days" but if you were from the masses of working class people, life was extremely hard by today's standards.

I would like to take this opportunity to thank all those people who have assisted me with this book. Firstly, all the staff at the BEVERLEY Public Library reference section, especially Miss Pam Martin, without whose assistance my endeavours would have been fruitless.

Also thanks to the Hull Public Library staff, Goole Times, Hull Daily Mail, East Yorkshire Newspapers Ltd., and not forgetting the staff of the long since defunct newspaper, the Howdenshire Chronicle, for, without their marvellous reporting, there would have been no "Clippings from the Past".

I must pay special thanks to my sister-in-law, Mrs. Elaine Bowman, for all her work in deciphering my scribbled notes and presenting them in a readable manuscript.

Special thanks must also go to Peter Robinson, author of East Riding Ghost Stories, etc., who gave me such advice and assistance at the outset, that it was inevitable I would complete this book. Thanks Peter. Thanks also to Paul Hesp and Alan Hotchin.

Finally, I am indebted to my wife Joyce, and children, Hayley, Philip and Gareth for their support and understanding during the past months whilst I have produced this book, "Clippings from the Past".

David Bowman

ACKNOWLEDGEMENTS

Photographs reproduced by kind permission of:-

Mr. Chris Peacock of Driffield;
Mr. John Warcup of Pocklington;
Hull Central Library;
North Yorkshire County Library
Mr. Ian Samuel of Pocklington

Chapter I

ALL ASPECTS OF LIFE

OPEN AIR BATHING – HULL

Open air bathing is practiced in Hull all the year round – winter and summer alike. One or two persons regularly visit the William Wright Dock every morning, and are only dissuaded from having a dip when they find it impossible to break the ice on the surface of the water.

— *January, 1895*

THE ELECTRIC LIGHT IN HULL

Thursday was the birthday of the Hull Corporation Electric Lighting Station in DAGGER LANE. When the works were two years old, the complete equipment of the station and service in 1893 cost £23,072 but so great has been the demand for the supply of the light that additions have been made to the plant and the total worth at the present time is about £40,000.

Councillor Holder states that the income from the station in its first year was £2,200 and last year at a lessened charge, £4,800.

January, 1895

SEASONAL BENEVOLENCE AT BISHOP WILTON

To alleviate the distress occasioned by the severe weather, Lady Sykes has given instructions that a large quantity of soup be made every other day, and given to all who may apply for it; Mrs. Elworth of the Fleece Inn, having kindly undertaken the work of distribution. Her ladyship has supplemented this gift with a quantity of coals, the distribution of which has energetically been taken up by Mr. Lett. All thanks to Lady Sykes.

February, 1895

CYCLISTS BALL AT POCKLINGTON

The third of their popular functions was brought off on Wednesday night in the Oddfellows Hall, when about 30 couples tripped the floor merrily to the music of Mr. Young's Quadrille Orchestra of Hull, well into the next day.

The programme embraced 22 dances, ranging from the waltz to the "giddy gallop".

January, 1895

PROPERTY SALE – POCKLINGTON

On Wednesday at the Oddfellows Hall, Pocklington, Mr R. M. English conducted one of the largest property sales that has been held in Pocklington for a long time.

Lots sold were as follows:-

– "The Fleece" Public House at Bishop Wilton, was knocked down to Messrs. R. Cattle and Co., brewers, for £1,200.

– "The Cross Keys" at Fridaythorpe, sold to Mr. C. Rose of Malton for £1,000.

– 1 acre 2 roods of arable land near to Fridaythorpe, purchased for £80 by a Malton farmer.

GEORGE TODD, GROCER, &c.

Tea & Coffee Specialist.

All the Premises Lighted by Electricity.

NEW PAVEMENT, POCKLINGTON

George Todd – Grocer circa 1899. Now Pavement Stores, Pocklington.
George Todd was my great grandfather.

The Grocery Stores,

New Pavement,

Pocklington.

George Todd is much obliged for your esteemed
remittance and has pleasure in enclosing herewith formal
acknowledgment.

Telephone:
18, Pocklington.

FORTH

Telegrams:
Todd, Grocer, Pocklington.

English's new Office on the left. The original English's Mill is in the centre –
the Post Office now stands where the mill and house on the right is

– Coach House and Granary, freehold, in Great George Street, Pocklington, sold to Mrs. A. J. Boyden for £120.

Several other land sales were made.

January, 1895

PROPERTY IMPROVEMENT AT POCKLINGTON

A great improvement has been effected in the appearance of Market Street, Pocklington, by the erection of new offices and warehouses for Mr. R. M. English in place of the former dilapidated premises which, from an architectural point of view, were anything but handsome. On the basement is a spacious and well lighted office, and also a sack room, whilst upstairs ample accommodation is afforded for warehousing purposes. The exterior is of red brick, with slate roofing. Mr. T. Grant was the builder.

May, 1896

NORTH EASTERN RAILWAY WORKS AT YORK

At a special meeting on January 26th, of the York City Council, a Mr. Brown pointed out that it was reported in the City that about 700 men in the employ of the North Eastern Railway Company were about to be removed to the North of the Country.

That would mean the removal of about 1500 children from the city. Alderman Wragg remarked that if 700 wagon builders were removed to the North, 700 carriage builders would be brought in to take their places. The rumours have been neither confirmed nor denied by the railway authorities.

January, 1895

EXPLOSION AT BEVERLEY

An explosion of gas took place on Monday night at the detached residence occupied by Mr. John Blithe in the rear of York Terrace. There was an escape of gas from the chandelier in the drawing room, and Mr. Blithe and his son took a lighted taper into the bedroom above and removed a floor board with the object of finding out the escape.

A quantity of gas had accumulated in the ceiling, and immediately the board was removed a loud explosion occurred in the room below. A large sheet of plate glass was blown from the window into the garden and the curtains and other articles were set on fire, damage being done to the amount of £10. Fortunately no one was in the room at the time.

February, 1895

DELAYED POST

Due to the weather the other day, a farmer in the High Wolds district of East Yorkshire had handed to him a packet of letters, the accumulation of three weeks, detailing the seizure, illness, dying condition and death and burial of his daughter, all of which, he had been in ignorance of.

March, 1895

DUSTMEN COMPLAIN – BRIDLINGTON

Complaints have been made that the residents do not rise early enough in the morning at Bridlington to unlock their doors for the dustmen. In one district 84 doors were found fast when the dustmen called. This does not arise from the residents being out. "Of course, the dustman unlike the train, wait for no man', and according to Councillor Sawden they are not able to wait knocking at one door a quarter of an hour.

July, 1895

SINGULAR FIND AT HOLME ON SPALDING MOOR

On Tuesday last, when the last train from Selby reached Holme, a young girl directed the notice of a porter to a parcel that was in a carriage. When examined the bundle was found to contain the body of a new born baby. The information was at once given to Inspector Jackson. An inquest was held on Wednesday, when a verdict of "found dead" was returned.

May, 1895

FIRE AT MARKET WEIGHTON

On Saturday morning, the foreman of Lord Londesborough's brickyard discovered that a fire had destroyed part of the machinery. None of the regular fires were going, and the fire of the driving engine, which is some distance away, was also extinguished. It is generally supposed that the fire originated in the canvas covering of the rollers, through the overheating of the machinery. It has thrown several men out of work.

August, 1895

A FOUL NUISANCE AT POCKLINGTON

The Sanitary Inspector, Mr. G. H. Gibson, referred to an alleged nuisance in connection with a house in Church Lane, Pocklington, based on the report of the Medical Officer of Health, Dr. Fairweather. On the 8th day of August, in company with the Sanitary Inspector, he examined an unoccupied house in Church Lane, situated at the end of Waterloo Terrace. He found the atmosphere inside very offensive and considered the premises, in their present state, to be unhealthy and unfit for human inhabitation. He will advise that the foundation soil of the building should be removed to a depth of two feet, as it was evidently much polluted, and that it be replaced by gravel or other suitable material. The drain in the yard should also be properly trapped. Councillor Cundall said the stench was intolerable. The doctor further reported that on the following day he examined an adjoining yard and found the drainage defective. It ought to be rectified, and the ash pits and privies should be more frequently cleared out.

August, 1895

MIRACULOUS ESCAPE FOR WARTER PLUMBER

Last Friday week the Warter Estate plumber, W. Noble, was attending to some of the windows at the top of the conservatory at Warter Priory, when his foot slipped and he went crashing through the plate glass and fell a distance of 15 feet. Fortunately he had the presence of mind to somewhat regulate his fall, by throwing his head backwards, otherwise he most certainly would have been killed on the spot. As it was, his head never came into collision with the stonework at all, but he was badly cut and bruised and Dr. Fairweather was summoned to attend the patient.

August, 1895

Warter Priory (Demolished about 1970)

11

EAST RIDING ASYLUM

The East Riding Asylum is to be increased in size so as to accommodate 100 more female patients. The estimated cost for the extensions is not to exceed £7,000. In 1890, the sum of £1,350 was voted, to enlarge the female wing of the establishment.

August, 1895

SHOCKING FATALITY AT BARMBY MOOR

A child killed by a reaper. – On Wednesday a most distressing accident happened at Barmby Moor, whereby a little girl, named Florence Mary Drury, aged 2 years, was robbed of her life. The little child, who was the daughter of Mr. James Drury, farmer, was playing in the field, and was hidden in the corn and tares. The reaper came up at the time and accidentally caught the poor little thing, and inflicted such terrible injuries that it succumbed shortly afterwards. One leg, we are informed, was severed in two places, and 3 fingers were cut off. The inquest will be heard this afternoon.

August, 1895

A HEALTH RISK AT POCKLINGTON

The Medical Officer occupied the house occupied by William Hotham, situated in Stathers Yard, and found it in a very dirty condition. The Medical Officer issued a certificate to destroy the whole of the bedding at once, on account of its filthy condition. I, therefore, had the bedding destroyed the same day, and the house swilled out with disinfectant, and Stathers' sister promised to clean the house thoroughly for him. It seems a great pity that landlords and agents are to be found, who, for the paltry sum of 1 shilling or 1s 3d a week, will let houses to persons of this class, whose proper abiding place is in the workhouse, where they would be kept clean. I will urge the Council to use the wide powers vested in them to make all landlords who encourage this class of tenant pay for the periodical cleaning of their places, which would cost more than the rent would come to, and have the effect of making landlords more careful in their selection of tenants.

– Surveyors Report
September, 1895

INQUEST TO REAPER DEATH

Dr. Fairweather said to the jury that the child was brought to him by the father and mother on Wednesday, at about 12 o'clock in the forenoon. The child was evidently in a dying condition, and lived only about 15 minutes. The right leg was completely severed just below the knee joint and also just above the ankle. Portions of three fingers on the left hand were missing. There was also a superficial wound on the right thigh. The wounds had bled profusely, and, although a small silk handkerchief had been thrown over the limb, no other means had been used to check the bleeding. The bleeding might have been checked a little by the bandage. He considered that death was due to haemorrhaging and shock to the system. The Coroner remarked that it was curious it had not occurred to the parents to tie the handkerchief tightly around the limb. After a brief deliberation, the jury returned a verdict in accordance with the medical evidence.

September, 1895

SHOCKING GUN ACCIDENT AT STORWOOD

On Saturday last, whilst Mr. Jennings, of Storwood, was out shooting in the Oak Tree fields, his gun went off accidentally, and the contents lodged in the back of his head, inflicting frightful injuries. Marvellous to relate that Mr. Jennings was able to walk back to the house, taking back with him a partridge that he had shot. He went to bed, and medical aid summoned immediately, and we are glad to say that the latest reports to his progress are reassuring.

September, 1895

SAD CASE AT BARMBY MOOR

Last Saturday, an inquest was held at Barmby Moor on the body of John Edmund D...., aged 12, who died at an early hour on Thursday morning. From the evidence adduced, it appeared that the boy had for a long time been a sufferer. The father was a widower and the children had been left a good deal to themselves, a relative from Pocklington going over once a week, and sometimes oftener, to clean up, etc. Mrs. Rogers, a shop-keeper, deposed to supplying the children with provisions to the order of the father. Dr. Leadman said that he had attended the mother of the deceased, who died in April, from Tubercular Consumption. Soon after, he attended the boy, John Edmund. Owing to the filthy conditions of the house and the neglected state of the children, he communicated with the Society for the Prevention of Cruelty to Children. Subsequently the boy was removed to the Workhouse, and he did not know that he had come out. On October 3rd the father asked for a certificate and said his son was dead. This he declined to give. He had made a post-mortem examination, and found that the boy was much distorted and emanciated. Both lungs were congested and one contained tubercles. Death was caused by chronic tubercular peritonitis of long standing, and in his opinion, nothing could have saved the boy, but his surroundings might have been more comfortable. The jury returned a verdict in accordance with the medical evidence, and the Coroner urged the father to make better provision for the children.

October, 1895

LIGHT AND REASON WANTED AT HOWDEN

Considerable fear has been expressed in Howden owing to the town being kept in darkness at night through a deadlock between the Parish Council and the Gas Company. The latter offered to light the lamps for £100, but the Council at its last meeting decided to give £90. The Company refused. Such a thing has never been known before and the inhabitants loudly complain.

October, 1895

DEATH OF AN OLD STANDARD AT MARKET WEIGHTON

Last Sunday, there passed away in Market Weighton, a very old and much respected resident in the person of James Sanderson. The deceased was one of the pioneers, who assisted in the building of the railway from Selby to Market Weighton and Beverley and, after which, he entered into the service of the North Eastern Railway Company, and for 30 years he was a most faithful servant. Some 8 years ago he received the pension from the Company and has since resided in one of their houses. His death is mourned by a large circle.

October, 1895

HOWDEN HIRINGS

The first statutes for the hiring of SERVANTS was held at Howden last Tuesday. There was a large attendance, especially of male servants. A good number of engagements were entered, and hiring was brisk. Boys' wages were from £7-£9, strong lads £10-£13, older lads, ploughboys £14-£16, more experienced young men £18-£22. Foremen were not very numerous, figures quoted as being £24-£26. The Town Hall was open for female servants, of whom the supply was below the demand, girls fit for useful general work hired readily at good wages from £10-£16; the number of female servants is much less than it used to be.

November, 1895

DEATH OF THE ONLY PETER

With regret we have to announce the Reverend Peter Mackenzie will not be able to fulfil his engagement at Pocklington next Wednesday. He has responded to a higher call, even Heavenly one. He died at Dewsbury from congestion of the lungs on Thursday evening, at the age of 71, by nature worth he rose from being a "pit laddie" to be a "foremost Divine", and his decease leaves a gap that will never be filled. To know him was to love and admire him.

November, 1895

Regent Street, Pocklington

CHRISTMAS BILLS
– a letter to the Weekly News, Pocklington

Sir,

Now that the Season for bills approaches, for bills as well as geese and turkeys, etc., I venture to suggest to tradesmen that it would greatly convenience the Public if they would all send us bills when they were due on the 1st January. The practice of late years has been to send bills at anytime between January and March, but when bills come perpetually dropping in week after week you never know when you have done with them! Tradesmen expect punctual payments, and why cannot they be as punctual in sending their bills.

I am sir, ONE WHO WANTS TO PAY HIS DEBTS.

December, 1895

A BRIGHT DAY FOR A BRIDLINGTON COUPLE

Mr. and Mrs. Kilburn, of St. John's Street, Bridlington, have been fortunate enough to secure the "TIT BITS" old age pension prize of £100. It has been obtained by receiving the largest number of votes, 13,517, from the subscribers of "TIT BITS". For the next year they will receive £2 per week. Not a few votes went from Pocklington and District.

December, 1895

SAD FATALITY AT SANCTON
– A GENEROUS JURY

An inquest was held at the Star Inn, Sanction, on Monday morning, before the East Riding Coroner, on the body of Charles Young, infant son of John and Margaret Young. It appeared from the evidence of the parents, that Mrs. Young engaged in washing, and that she removed a pan of boiling water from the fire and placed it near the fender. She then left it for two or three minutes to attend to other duties and immediately after she was horrified to find the child in the pan of water. She at once lifted him out, and Dr. Jefferson was called in, but the child died soon after. The jury returned a verdict of accidental death and also very generously handed their fees to the parents of the deceased.

January, 1896

MARKET WEIGHTON PROVISIONS MARKET

Wednesday – Butter 1/- per lb, Eggs 13 for 1/-, Hens 3/- per couple, Chickens 3s-6d per couple, Ducks 5/- per couple, Pigeons 6/- per dozen, Hares 3/- to 4/- each, Wood Pigeons 7/- per dozen, Rabbits 2s-4d per couple

January, 1896

FOOTBALL SOCIAL EVENING – POCKLINGTON

With a view to replenishing the treasury chest, the Committee of the Pocklington Rugby Club have arranged to hold a social evening in the Oddfellows Hall, Pocklington. The first part of the evening will be devoted to harmony, for which a number of popular lyric artistes have promised their assistance, after which a dance will be held, as Nelsons Celebrated Dance Orchestra has been engaged. Lovers of the terpsichorean art will thus be able to indulge in their favourite pastime to their hearts delight.

– Admission concerts, front seats, 1/-, second seats 6d.

Dance 6d extra

Refreshments at moderate charges.

January, 1896

CHARITY DISTRIBUTION AT MARKET WEIGHTON

On Tuesday, at the Girls' School, Hungate, about 60 of the deserving poor widows and widowers of Market WEighton received LARGESSES of 3/- and 2s.6d. from the BLACKBURN and BREIGHTON Charities. The vicar dispensed the bounties.

February, 1896

STAMFORD BRIDGE MAGIC LANTERN SHOW

On Wednesday night, a magic lantern entertainment was given in the school room, under the auspices of the CHURCH of ENGLAND TEMPERANCE SOCIETY, the proceeds of which were in aid of the reading room. The series of slides consisted of "The Wreck of the Hesperus", "Views of London", "Temperance Statistics", "The Wonderful Telescope" and views of various places of interest around the World. A few comic pictures were thrown in on the screen for the younger people present. There was only a fair attendance.

March, 1896

BICYCLES FOR EAST RIDING POLICEMEN

The quarterly meeting of the Standing Joint Committee was held at Beverley, when the tender of Messrs. Shepherdson of Driffield, was accepted for the new Police Station, at £2,659. It was also decided to spend not exceeding £180 on the purchase of 12 bicycles for the use of the police, one for each Petty Sessional Division.

April, 1896

EYES RIGHT – POCKLINGTON

F. COMPANY V.B. EAST YORKSHIRE REGIMENT. 3rd Class firing will take place at the Pocklington range on Monday, May 25th, at 5 pm. Best tunics to be worn on Wednesday, for drill, and second tunics on Saturday, May 30th. Wednesday 27th, drill 7.15 pm in Mr. Thirsk's field. Every member of the corps must draw his greatcoat from the armoury sometime before drill Saturday 30th, parade at 5 pm sharp in Mr. Thirsk's field, for march out, returning to Pocklington at noon on Sunday. Drill order. Greatcoats to be brought rolled up in bundles.

May, 1896

ACCOUNTS – POCKLINGTON SCHOOL

The Headmaster of the Pocklington Grammar School requests that the tradespeople of the town will not allow the boys to run up credit accounts. He will only be responsible for goods for which a written order, signed by himself, is given.

June, 1896

MISSING CERTIFICATE
– Singular incident at Pocklington Wedding

On Tuesday afternoon a local couple, from the Country, were about to be united by the ties of matrimony at the Wesleyan Chapel, Pocklington, and when all was in residence, the bridegroom found, to his dismay, that he had forgotten to bring his certificate. It appeared that he had left it in the pocket of another coat. What was to be done? Time was fleeting, and, of course, the function could not take place without the all important document, which was now lying at one of the adjacent villages. Happy thought! – a bicycle was promptly commissioned to seek that which was lost. He accomplished his errand in good time and, after a rather embarrassing wait, the happy couple were married by the Reverand William James and sent on their way rejoicing.

June, 1896

A SIGN OF THE TIMES

Of the 46 persons who signed the register of death certificates during the last quarter, only 1 had to make a cross. This is the lowest percentage of illiteracy which has occurred in the Pocklington District since Mr. Fowler became Registrar of Births and Deaths.

July, 1896

AN ESCAPED LUNATIC

A letter was read from the East Riding Asylum stating that a patient from Pocklington, named Loften, had escaped and had not been recovered. Mr. M. Fowler, Relieving Officer, said the man was a tramp, and his escape would relieve the Union of further expense.

August, 1896

LIGHTNING STRIKE – HOLME

A farmer, named Thomas Smith, of Holme, was SWATHE- RAKING, when he was struck by lightning. His boots were torn off his feet, and his watch melted. His clothing took fire and had to be extinguished by buckets of water. He is now progressing favourably.

September, 1896

COOKERY LECTURES – POCKLINGTON

The above mentioned lectures have been so eminently successful at Pocklington this season that two classes have had to be arranged instead of one per evening, and now no more pupils can be admitted. A public demonstration took place at the Oddfellows Hall on Tuesday night, when an audience of about 50 persons, heard, saw, and were edified.

October, 1896

AMBULANCE CLASSES – POCKLINGTON

At Pocklington on Tuesday evening, the first of a series of homely lectures on the principles and practice of St. John's Ambulance was held in the waiting room at the Pocklington Railway Station. There were some 22 people present, including some railwaymen from Pocklington, Fangfoss, etc., and a sprinkling of the general public. The practical address of Dr. Angus Fairweather was listened to with great interest. The lectures are promoted by the North Eastern Railway Company.

November, 1896

PROPOSED PUBLIC HALL FOR MARKET WEIGHTON

On Tuesday night at a meeting of the Parish Council in Market Weighton, Mr. Hollings, presiding, decided to call a ratepayers meeting on the 17th November, to consider the desirability or otherwise of erecting a Public Hall for the town, there being at present no accommodation in that respect.

November, 1896

TYROLESE TROUBADORS AT POCKLINGTON

On Thursday night, at the Oddfellows Hall, this excellent company commenced 4 days visit. There was a good audience present and the various items were received with much applause. The entertainment, which consisted of dioramics, songs, jokes, choruses, dancing, and selections on various musical instruments, hand bells, concluded with a short sketch. Bumper houses should be the rule.

November, 1896

Mr. Sawyers, a North Cave postman, has travelled 150,476 miles in 26 years in pursuing his calling.

November, 1896

POCKLINGTON CONSERVATIVE CLUB

Opening of new premises – The acquisition of spacious premises by the Conservative Club was, on Monday, made the occasion of an interesting function in which the member for the division and a large muster of the Conservative Liberal

Unionists from the Division participated. The new premises are in **Railway Street**, and include a commodious billiards room, reading room, extensive yard and caretaker's apartments. On the ground floor, there is a committee room, recreation room and secretary's office. The rooms are heated with slow combustion stoves, and are well lighted and comfortably appointed.

December, 1896

WATCH FOUND AT WARTER

After many days, whilst two men were repairing the roof of a cottage at Warter Village a few days ago, they found a gold watch under one of the ridgeing stones. It was little the worse for its adventure, and upon inspection it was found to be the property of Mrs. C. H. Wilson, of Warter Priory. It is 12 years since the watch was missed. The finders were handsomely rewarded by Mrs. Wilson.

December, 1896

NOTICE FROM YAPHAM

Notice is hereby given that I, John Johnson of Yapham, will not be responsible from this date for debts incurred by my wife Evelyn Johnson – Yapham 17th December, 1896.

December, 1896

QUAKE OF THE EARTH AT POCKLINGTON

In common with other portions of England, though, happily not to such an extent, a distinct seismic shock was experienced on Thursday morning, at about 5.30 am in the Pocklington district. One person in the town who was awake at the time, not only felt a vibration which made the bed shake, but noticed a slight rumbling which accompanied the unwanted disturbance. The servant maid in the house likewise felt the shocks. Of course, at the breakfast table, any suggestion of an earthquake was otherly scouted, but those who had felt the shock could not be moved in their belief, and yesterday's newspaper report of a seismic disturbance of so general a character that they almost amounted to corroborative evidence.

December, 1896

INDIAN FAMINE FUND

A collection in aid of the Indian Famine Fund was taken at Melbourne Church last Sunday evening.

At the request of Lord Herries, the York Union Bank has consented to receive subscriptions on behalf of the Indian Famine Fund, promoted by the Lord Lieutenants of the County, and any subscriptions from this district may be paid to York Union Bank.

February, 1897

POCKLINGTON CHURCH RESTORATION FUND

Restoration funds swelled by £30 – On Wednesday afternoon a sale of work in aid of the funds for the much needed restoration of the Parish Church, was held in the National School. In order to complete restoration of the "grand old pile" £6,000 is computed to be required, towards which £170 has been raised, and the immediate object of the effort to the notice was to provide the where withall for restoring the bent column in the left aisle as a prime necessity.

February, 1897

POCKLINGTON AND THE DIAMOND JUBILEE

On Monday evening at the Oddfellows Hall, Pocklington, a large, enthusiastic, and thoroughly representative audience met together with a view to considering what steps should be taken to mark the Diamond Jubilee of our Gracious Sovereign, Queen Victoria.

Briefly the Chairman gave a brief resum of what was decided upon 10 years ago, when a meeting was convened by the late Admiral Duncombe, and the unanimous resolution was passed to celebrate the Queen's Golden Jubilee. A large committee had been formed and the town was mapped out into districts and properly canvassed. So committees were again formed and he suggested that what was done in 1887 would have to be done now.

The first thing was to decide whether something should be done in the way of celebrating the Diamond Jubilee, and then to appoint a thoroughly representative committee to carry the arrangements through. Ten years ago £101 15s 1d was raised, of which £100 8s 8d was spent and the balance divided amongst the three day schools in Pocklington. Any question as to the detail he should be glad to give and the papers in connection with the 1887 Jubilee are in his possession and it would be his pleasure and privilege to give every information in his power.

Councillor Cundall rose to propose the first resolution and said that they were all living in a Glorious Age, and under a Queen, who as a wife, mother or widow had gained Golden opinions and during her reign had been in the van of progress and civilisation, Mistress of the Seas, and he might say the World. He proposed that the inhabitants of Pocklington be invited to subscribe to a fund to be applied to celebrating and commemorating Her Majesty's Diamond Jubilee.

Councillor R. M. English next proposed that a committee be appointed to collect subscriptions and to decide on the exact mode of celebrating and commemorating and to carry out necessary arrangements.

It was suggested that ornamental trees be planted in various parts of the town as a permanent memorial. Councillor Cundall suggested that on the Sunday there should be a special, fully choral thanksgiving service in the Church, when there should be a parade in which the members of the Urban Council and the Volunteers might join.

The building of the public swimming baths had been mentioned but the cost of £1,000 seemed to be too much. Mr. Fielder suggested that the Parish Church clock might be illuminated.

A capital and memorable meeting was brought to an end by a hearty vote of thanks to the Chairman.

April, 1897

JUBILEE

As a tribute to Her Majesty's Diamond Jubilee, the tradespeople of Pocklington suggested that a Public Hall be built with a public swimming pool constructed beneath it.

April, 1897

SAD CASE OF POCKLINGTON CHOIR BOY

Early yesterday morning William Skinn, 13, died from tetanus (lock jaw). It is alleged that the young lad died from injuries received during a game of cricket on the piece of turf at the Mile End 10 days ago. An inquest will be held this afternoon. The deceased was a considerate boy who attended the Wesleyan day school and sang in the Parish Church choir.

From the latest information it is stated that a wicket was thrown at SKINN, and the point of it caused a punctured wound on the right temple. Nothing serious was anticipated until a week after the accident when the first symptoms of lock jaw appeared which proved fatal in the course of 24 hours.

June, 1897

INQUEST INTO SKINN ACCIDENT

It was stated that after a fight amongst the young players, a wicket was thrown at the head of William Skinn. Dr. Fairweather had examined the victim and discovered at the post mortem examination that the wound had penetrated through the skull and into the brain. The skull was fractured and the wound was a punctured one with effusion outside. The cause of death was tetanus, due to the wound not being thoroughly cleaned, and lack of disinfectant. It was probable that there was some earth on the wicket. The Coroner, in summing up, said that it was his opinion that this was not a case of manslaughter but of misadventure. The jury returned a verdict of death from tetanus, caused by a wound to the head. They expressed their sympathy with the relatives and acquitted them of all possible neglect in the matter of cleansing and disinfecting the wound, as they appeared to be quite ignorant of its seriousness.

June, 1897

CAPTIVE BALLOON – A GREAT SUCCESS
– BRIDLINGTON

The captive balloon proved a great success with the visitors on Whit Monday. The first ascent was at 11 am – a charge of 2s 6d per person was made. So great was the desire on the part of the spectators to ascend that at the end of the day the receipts stood at £70.

The inflation of the balloon was attended with some inconvenience to worshippers in various Chapels and Churches on Sunday night. Just as the choir at Holy Trinity Church had finished singing a hymn – the last of which runs "let there be light" the gas went out and the manager of the Gas Works who was present was suddenly deprived of the spiritual benefit of the service.

June, 1897

WORLDS LARGEST BALLOON LOST – BRIDLINGTON

The captive balloon, which has been for sometime working at the new Spa, Bridlington, and which is the largest in the world, broke loose from its moorings on Thursday in the high winds which have steadily been increasing. Fortunately the wire rope attached to the balloon held, but there was for a time a great danger of the engine that controlled it being pulled up and down the embankment.

A gun was sent for in great haste to shoot the balloon, so as to let out the gas, but before it arrived the whole thing collapsed into the sea. It was, however, secured. Considerable loss was ensured to Messrs. Whittaker Bros. It is presumed that, not expecting the high winds, there had not been sufficient ballast put into the balloon.

The affair caused a great deal of excitement in the town, hundreds of people watching the proceedings.

June, 1897

BALLOON TO BE REPLACED – BRIDLINGTON
The captive balloon which came to grief in the terrific gale last week is to be replaced by one not quite so large, but it will be just as strong, and will have a carrying capacity of 8 to 10 persons.

June, 1897

BALLOON FLIGHTS AT BRIDLINGTON
Visitors to Bridlington wishing to take aerial flights are waiting patiently for a change of wind. Although the new balloon has been made perfectly safe, there seems to exist a feeling that the Accidental Insurance Office would regard flight in the present high wind as extra hazardous.

July, 1897

NEW BALLOON AT BRIDLINGTON
The new balloon at Bridlington has made several aerial ascents. The sensational was tried last, by a bank clerk, who went up with the attendant. This balloon does not maintain a perfect perpendicular position, as the last one. It ascends as smoothly as anyone can wish, but it travels in a slightly slanting position. It is now being put through the "DRESSING" operation, and in a day or two will again be in full swing.

July, 1897

NEW SPA – BRIDLINGTON
The new Spa at Bridlington is going to celebrate its birthday on Monday, Messrs. Brock having designed special fireworks. They will make most effective use of the miniature lakes in its grounds by designs of boats, swans, comic acrobats and other humorous devices.

July, 1897

HULL TO BRIDLINGTON TELEPHONE LINE
The final step towards establishing TELEPHONIC COMMUNICATION between Hull and Bridlington will take place this week. It is expected that by Thursday, subscribers to the National Telephone system at Hull would be able to speak to subscribers at Bridlington, and visitors there would be able to speak from the call offices.

July, 1897

DUST IN THE STREETS – WITHERNSEA
The dust in the streets has been simply abominable. The water cart has certainly been out for a day or two but what is the use if the dust on the roads is never swept up and carted away? The roads were certainly better looked after before the

beginning of the season than they are now. I am told that the roadman has had the Irishmans pay rise – from 3s to 2s 6d per day, and consequently he takes any other job he can get at a greater remunerative price, and quite right too, 2s 6d per day is not a living wage in a seaside resort like Withernsea, where rents are much higher than in surrounding villages.

If Withernsea is to prosper she must, and quickly, have her own Board to direct her own affairs and not be under the control of a body of about 30, mostly farmers, who sit once a fortnight at Patrington, and do know and care very little what its requirements are.

June, 1897

POLICE – HULL

The length of streets, alleys, squares and roads patrolled by the Hull Police is 107 miles. The nett cost of the Force last year was £26,347 being at the rate of £87 4s 10d per Officer.

June, 1897

FOREIGN LUNATICS IN HULL

A curiosity in British law enables foreign pauper lunatics to land at Hull or any other British ports, where they immediately become chargeable to the rates.

If these persons are sent back to their native land the authorities will not permit them to go ashore, and so they come back again. We have now in the Hull Asylum two Russian lunatics and a Swedish woman.

The Mayor pressed the Corporation Asylum Committee this afternoon to ask the Swedish Consul to remove the woman from the chargeability of the Hull rates. He, and Alderman Toozers, were of one opinion – that nothing would be obtained unless an effort were made.

June, 1897

HULL FARRIERS UP IN ARMS

The Hull farriers are up in arms against "their sea of troubles". Last night Mr. C. Midddleton presided at a meeting protesting against the Hull Town Council adopting the electric tram scheme.

June, 1897

CORSETS – HULL

The number of women who now walk the streets of Hull without corsets is increasing.

June, 1897

BOMB SCARE – GOOLE

Quite a scene was witnessed in the Old Customs House by the appearance of a suspicious looking package, which had been deposited in one of the rooms.

Certain circumstances led the officials to suppose that the package was an "INFERNAL MACHINE", and that a plot had been laid for the destruction of the Customs and for the wholesale extinction of Her Majesty's Customs Officials at Goole. Hurried consultations were held, the room in the meantime being evacuated, and the police were communicated with. Several officers appeared on the scene, and the mysterious parcel was carefully removed to the Police Station, great care being taken to prevent oscillation. Here it was drenched with buckets of water, and eventually an Officer summoned up courage, unfastened the parcel, and carefully removed the wrappings of soft paper to find at last an innocent looking piece of glass.

It is now believed a practical joker is amongst those "wanted".

June, 1897

DEATH FROM A THORN – SANCTON

Mrs. Cox, a widow from Sancton, near Market Weighton, died quite suddenly in the street yesterday. It seems that for a few days she had been suffering from the effect of a thorn prick, and whilst out yesterday the sore had commenced to bleed, and in a quarter of an hour the woman had bled to death.

July, 1897

POST OFFICE – BRIDLINGTON

Bridlington with all its vaunted glory and importance, is not yet a place to be trusted with the responsibility of a post office. At present the offices are "SUB" off Leeds. Another point raised is that the post office, or whatever it is, is now located at the back of a chemists shop in the Old Town. So that visitors and others at the Quay, whose letters are addressed Bridlington, when they require immediate attention, must walk a mile and a half to fetch them. Representations upon the kindness and generosity of the post office in London for a better arrangement.

July, 1897

Note: This picture was taken before the Hull City Hall was built

24

SKIDDING ON THE WET GROUND – HULL

To the editor –

Sir, may I occupy a small space in your valuable paper, in order to second "a disgusted traveller" in his endeavour to put a stop to the great inconvenience and annoyance caused by the excessive watering of the streets in the centre of the City.

Speaking from experience as a cyclist, I have found it positively dangerous to ride through the centre of the City after the streets have been watered, having been several times thrown from my machine owing to the wheels skidding on the wet ground. Knowing that some of the gentlemen holding office in the City are cyclists themselves, I trust they will do what they can to see that this great evil is stopped. You will notice, I refer to the excessive use of the water cart. I am Sir,

Cyclist.

July, 1897

DEAD SALMON

Several dead salmon were observed in the River Ouse near BOOTHFERRY, on Sunday. They had possibly got too near the River Aire, and been poisoned by the dye water.

July, 1897

ROWDY BRIDLINGTON?

There has been a report that on Saturday, excursionists at Bridlington were noisy and disorderly. Superintendent Harvey, on the other hand declared, that the people on the most part might be termed, a comparatively well behaved lot. There were about 6,000 on the sands. Excursionists of this sort are not such as leave much behind with the tradesmen. They mostly pursue pleasures with a frugal mind. They bring sandwiches in a satchel, and leave much paper behind.

It is sometime since Bridlington was known as Sheffield by the Sea. Sheffield people have in recent times gone to Cleethorpes, and Bridlington makes up for this by receiving thousands of Hull trippers.

July, 1897

FIRE ENGINE – BRIDLINGTON

One would think that one of the first things a town will do when it gets its Incorporation capitalised, will be to get a fire engine. The Old Town looks a dreary and Godforsaken place and, supposing a fire was to break out, there would be great danger of a great conflagration. One might get out the manual equipment, but while they are fiddling, getting voluntary assistance, and wiring Scarborough, "The stable might be burning". As of now there is but one man in charge of the fire appliance.

July, 1897

VENDORS AT WITHERNSEA

Go down the beautiful and attractive seaside road any excursion day, what do you see. Foreign ice-cream carts, hokey pokey sellers, hot pea vendors, rulleys, with scores of boxes of aerated waters on the pavement, blocking the way to the promenade, and anywhere and everywhere to suit their own convenience, not caring one jot for the other Withernsea Vendors who have to pay rates, for the convenience of the visitors, who only sell their merchandise.

July, 1897

GAS WORKS – DRIFFIELD

The Gas Works have been taken over at last. The Treasurer to the Council received a cheque for £22,500 on Thursday morning, and a couple of hours later the money was transferred to the debit side of the new gas account. This is the biggest thing in cheques lately in the town, and the shareholders in the Gas Company can now clap their hands with the completion of the "bargain". The ratepayers it is said have got a "millstone" around their necks.

July, 1897

PRESERVE THE SABBATH – HULL

Hull barbers are "up in arms" against the practice which several "tonsorial artists" have adopted by opening their establishments on Sundays.

It is pointed out that several of those who are not satisfied with the ordinary working week do not even close on Thursday afternoon. A determined effort is to be made to preserve the Sabbath.

July, 1897

Chapter II

ANIMALS

CATTLE MARKET AT MARKET WEIGHTON

There was a large attendance of buyers and farmers but trade was dull. BEEF made 6/- to 6s 9d per stone, MUTTON maintained its high price, 8d to 9d per lb, pigs were a very poor show. Some useful porkers made 5/- per stone.

January, 1895

SHARKS AT BRIDLINGTON

Sharks have been seen at Bridlington. The excitement of the Bridlington fishermen was at a high temperature, as might almost have been expected, for an army of sharks would undoubtedly have cleared the Bay of fish stocks.

It is stated that some visitors first spotted the monsters of the deep. The opinion is not unanimous upon the question of whether the creatures were of that denomination or whether they belong to a large sort of the Porpoise species, which are often seen in the Bay from the end of the pier, especially in squally weather. Anyway, the fishermen are going on their way rejoicing.

July, 1895

SINGULAR DEATH OF A HORSE AT MARKET WEIGHTON

On Monday night, a son of Mr. Bridge of Market Weighton, went into a field near the Red House, with the purpose of bringing away a calf. He got the calf into the trap when the horse began to kick, and eventually ran into the next field, where it dropped down dead. The loss will be a serious one to the owner, as he had sold the horse, which was to be delivered the next day. It was not insured.

August, 1895

FAT STOCK SHOW AT CHRISTMAS

Fatstock show at Pocklington – a fine display

The Pocklington Christmas fat stock show sale was held in the auction mart adjoining the Buck Hotel, on Tuesday, when prizes to the value of £20 were given by the auctioneer, Mr. R. M. English, and the tradesmen of Pocklington. The show this year was an excellent one, being the best that has been held for years. There were 44 beasts, 150 sheep, and 224 pigs. The beasts were a very good lot and sold well, the best realising 8s. per stone.

December, 1895

VISITING COW – MARKET WEIGHTON

At a farmhouse near MARKET WEIGHTON, a cow coolly walked in uninvited and managed to get into one of the bedrooms. Wonderful to relate, the unwelcome and uninvited visitor was ejected without any damage being done.

July, 1896

REMARKABLE SCENE AT THE POCKLINGTON CANAL

On the Pocklington Canal yesterday, a tragic tussle was witnessed between the 4th and 5th locks, when a splendid Dog Otter was observed to land a huge pike onto the canal bank. The fish made vigorous attempts to regain its native element, and actually flapped its way back into the water, but its foe knew no truce, and seizing the pike, brought it to land again. Then began a battle some three quarters of an hour, the fish eventually succumbing to the terrific onslaught of the "VARMINT". On being disturbed, the otter made speedy tracks, and the fish was carried to Pocklington where it turned the scales at 14 lbs, and measured 1 yard in length, with a circumference of 17 inches.

October, 1896

HORSE COMMITS SUICIDE – GOOLE

It is very seldom that a horse has been known to have committed suicide but such cases have been heard of. One occurred as late as this week, at WHITGIFT, near Goole. From the animal demeanor it was evidently insane. It commenced attacking another horse and when it was ultimately got away from this, it set about revenging itself on the man. Fortunately, however he escaped with little or no injury, but the animal, who by this time became extremely vicious, jumped some railings by the river bank and made a bolt for the water. After considerable trouble it was brought onto terra firma, but a few minutes later it repeated its performance and was drowned.

July, 1897

Chapter III

TRANSPORT AND ACCIDENTS

A STEAM PILOT CUTTER LAUNCHED AT BEVERLEY

Steam is destined to supplant the old fashioned sailing cutter. Following the example by London, theHome pilots have just introduced a new steam vessel and should it prove the success it is anticipated, others will probably be added. The vessel, which was launched on Tuesday at Messrs. Cochrane and Coopers Yard, Beverley, is a splendid model, and took to the water in a gratifying manner. She was named the "W. A. MASSEY" by Miss Massey, daughter of the Chairman of the Pilotage Commissioners, who has interested himself largely in promoting the "Humber Pilots Steam Cutter Company". After the ceremony the Company were entertained by the builders to breakfast.

January, 1895

OMNIBUS

In a certain town in the North of the Riding, a travelling American found an omnibus which carried First, Second, and Third Class passengers. As the seats were all alike, the traveller was mystified but not for very long. Midway along the route the omnibus stopped at the foot of a large, steep hill, and the guard shouted, "First Class passengers keep your seats. Second Class passengers please get out and walk. Third Class passengers get out and push".

January, 1895

H.M.S. SALMON LAUNCHED AT HULL

H.M.S. Salmon, the first of an order of two of the new type of vessels, known in the Service as "TORPEDO BOAT DESTROYERS", was launched on Tuesday from the yard of Earle's Shipbuilding and Engineering Company, Hull. The Ship is 200 feet long, between perpendiculars, and 19 feet 6 inches broad, while the design draft of water is only 5 feet 6 inches. These vessels unusual proportions being rendered necessary for the extraordinary speed of 25 knots (over over 31 statute miles per hour). To accomplish the phenomenal speed she is fitted with twin screw engines on the triple expansion principle, which are to make rather more than 6 revolutions every second, and develop 4,000 indicated horsepower, or more than is required to drive a large Atlantic Cargo Liner at full speed. When the ship was put into water she was practically complete, with engines and boilers on board, and she was subsequently berthed in the Alexandria Dock, where she will make final preparations for the official test. The trial of the machinery under steam is taking place sometime during the present week. A sister ship, H.M.S. SNAPPER, will be launched in a few days time.

January, 1895

FLAMBOROUGH LIFEBOAT DAMAGED

A Flamborough correspondent writes, "On Monday morning the lifeboat "MATTHEW MIDDLEWOOD" stationed at the South Landing, was launched at 9.30 am and proceeded to a schooner three miles off shore, from which it was reported a flag of distress was flying. It was half ebb and, as the lifeboat has not a carriage, it was no easy thing to secure a good launch to face the breakers. The lifeboat in going off took a tremendous sea, which smashed several oars. The four spare oars were unlashed and fixed, and the brave fellows pulled hard to the schooner. On reaching her it was found that what had been taken as a signal of distress was the part of a torn sail in the shape of a flag. The vessel proved to be the "FLIRT" of Newcastle. The crew would not leave the vessel, though she was in a terrible plight on account of the gale. The crew were working hard at the pumps. The lifeboat crew stated "if the weather gets worse the Captain will have to beach his vessel". Further disaster occurred to the lifeboat on returning to the shore. The tide being down made it difficult to land. When quite near the shore, a heavy sea broke into her broadside and threw the boat on the leeside. smashing six oars. Thus the ten oars in numbers for active service were broken, leaving the four spare oars only available for use.

January, 1895

FATALITY ON A HULL TUG

– INQUEST

At the Friendly Society, Hull, on Wednesday, before Mr. A. Thorney, deputy coroner, an inquest was held on the body of Tom Patrick. Mr. Thorney said the deceased was the mate on the steam tug "JAMES WATT", which at about 8 am on Saturday, was comiing down the river from Keadby. Patrick picked up a single barrel gun, loaded with No. 6 shot, which was lying on a coil of rope. The rope caught the trigger of the gun, which went off, and the charge lodged in Patrick's right arm. He was taken to Hull Infirmary and doctors subsequently found it necessary to amputate the arm, but he did not survive the operation by more than 36 hours.

– Dr. Sutcliffe, house surgeon at the Infirmary, said that the deceased was admitted at 11 am on Saturday and amputation was at once performed, but Patrick never rallied from the shock, and died about 4 pm Sunday. Deceased evidently had a great loss of blood. A verdict of accidental death was returned.

February, 1895

NARROW ESCAPE ON THE RAILWAY – HESSLE

On Saturday morning, Mr. George Sneeston was crossing the line at Hessle Junction with a horse and rulley, property of his father, when the horse in some way got one of its shoes fast in the metals and fell, completely blocking the up and down lines. At the same time a goods train coming into Hull was signalled. The signalman in the box near, on perceiving the obstacle, immediately put the signal back and was only just in time to check almost suredly what would have resulted in the destruction of both horse and rulley. The engine driver had barely time to draw up, for the locomotive glided gently into the rulley and dragged it a few yards, bringing the horse along with it. However, the train was brought to a standstill before any serious damage was done, and Mr. Sneeston feels thankful that he escaped with only a slight cut on the hand and a severe fright. The horse is little the worse for its escapade.

February, 1895

WAGGONETTES – HULL

There are 425 licenced waggonettes in Hull and it will be admitted that this number is far in excess of what it ought to be. There is an evident disposition on the part of the Hackney Carriage Committee not to issue new licences.

February, 1895

HORSE KILLED BY BEES

An extraordinary accident occurred near Scarborough on Wednesday. Three rulley loads of beehives full of bees, were being conveyed from the station at Sherburn. When near Sherburn the horses attached to the foremost rulley stumbled on the rough road, and caused the topmost hive to fall on its back. The bees swarmed out of the hive and onto the back of the horse, which was stung so badly that it plunged and bolted. The rulley was broken and the bees from the nine hives were liberated and they swarmed onto the horse and driver literally covering them. The animal plunged so violently that it too broke away from the cart, and dashing away ran into a wall, killing itself instantly. The driver and a boy were so severelty stung that they had to be medically treated.

March, 1895

TRAM ACCIDENT – HULL

Yesterday afternoon a tram coming along Whitefriargate, ran into a "HOKEY POKEY" cart. The boy who was in charge of it was on the lines at the time. After the contents of the cart were strewn about, the boy was heard to say, "A Jew has stolen 6d – six penny worth it". Luckily there were no injuries.

July, 1895

THE CHANNEL FLEET AT SCARBOROUGH

The Channel Squadron is to arrive at the Scarborough Roadstead at breakfast time. £350 has been promised by public subscriptions and both Officers and Men are to be feted. In return, the Public, weather permitting, be allowed free access to the Men o' War. The fleet departs on Wednesday next.

During the stay of the Channel Fleet at Scarborough, 54,000 people are computed to have visited the war vessels. Many visitors travelled by special excursion trains from the East Riding.

September, 1895

KILLED BY A TRACTION ENGINE – POCKLINGTON

A shocking accident, which terminated fatally, occurred to Edward Kettlewell, aged 67. The deceased was engaged as a flagman to a traction engine, driven by Mr. T. Prentice. About 6 o'clock at night, the engine was on the road and the deceased was walking 20 yards in front of it. On turning a corner near the railway station, the driver had noticed the flagman had stopped and before it was possible to shut off steam, the front wheel was upon him. At the inquest held, before Mr. Henry Woods, yesterday, it was stated in evidence that the deceased had been subject to fainting fits, and had had one two days previously to the accident. The driver called to Kettlewell but he appeared to fall and he received such injuries that he died in a very few minutes. At the time of the accident, the engine was only travelling at the rate of 3 miles per hour. As the deceased's tobacco was found by his side, it is conjectured that he stopped to light his pipe and had a fit. The jury found that he was accidentally killed.

September, 1895

Chapmangate, Pocklington

VEHICULAR COLLISION AT POCKLINGTON

A very awkward coincidence happened on Tuesday night. Dr. A. Fairweather was being driven by his coachman, Mr. Belt, to the scene of a trap accident, whither he had been summoned to give medical assistance, and when opposite Mr. Gibson's shop in the Market Place, Pocklington, a collision took place between their trap and another one. Dr. Fairweather speedily realised the position and jumped out, but his coachman remained in the trap, which was completely turned round and the shafts damaged. Fortunately, Belt was not injured. The other trap retained its balance andthe driver drove away.

December, 1895

THE ROADS
– a letter to the editor of the Weekly News, Pocklington

Dear Sir,

Will you kindly find a corner in your paper on the above subject and the consequent cruelty to animals. The roads are in a very bad state and are not fit for a horse to travel on. In some places they are so bad that we have to travel on the sides of the road to get a track for the horses. Stones are put where they are not wanted. The water had better be let off the middle of the roads, which should not be kept so low.

Alfred Wilson
Yapham Mill

December, 1895

West Green Crossing - Pocklington

A HORSE THAT GALLOPED FROM SHIPTON

Not a little sensation was caused on Wednesday night by a horse, with a trap attached, galloping from Shipton to Pocklington, with no one in charge. The animal, a valuable mare, belonged to a commercial traveller, and on its own responsibility came careering madly to Pocklington. On arriving at the railway gates its onward course was stopped, so it simply turned round, cantered off, and eventually walked into the stable yard of Mr. Simpson's, New Red Lion Hotel. That no mishap occurred was a marvel.

December, 1895

GOOD NEWS – REDUCTION IN RAILWAY RATES – POCKLINGTON

On Wednesday evening, notification was received at Pocklington, of an experimental material reduction in the Railway rates for the transit of agricultural stuffs, etc. The reductions have not been based on any parsimonious or niggardly scale, but have been designed as a substantial concession which should be considerably encouraged for the transit of agricultural produce to Leeds and to facilitate the conveyance of town MANURES to the country, where they can be used to the best advantage.

Rates – Grain, Packed MANURES, OIL CAKE, BEANS, PEAS, MACE, VEGETABLES.

A sweeping concession has been made, formerly the cost of 4 Ton loads to Leeds from Pocklington was 7s. 1d. and now the cost for 5 Ton loads is 6s. 3d.

MANURES and GAS LIMES – what formerly cost 2s. 6d. from Hull to Pocklignton is now 2s. 3d.

SHEEP – a medium truck of sheep formerly cost £1-6-3d from Pocklington to Leeds; now it will be 19s. 9d.

North Eastern Railways hope and trust that the easier rates will mean increased traffic.

January, 1896

A BREAKDOWN ON THE RAILWAY AT FANGFOSS

On Monday evening, travellers by the York train, timed to be at Fangfoss at 5-22 pm, had an unexpected experience. Owing to an accident to some of the brake gear and steam pipes of the engine, the train was detained for an hour. Several of the passengers walked to Pocklington. Ultimately the engine was temporarily repaired, and the train was able to proceed on its journey.

January, 1896

SENSATIONAL ACCIDENT AT POCKLINGTON
A horse dashes into express – miraculous escape

On Wednesday afternoon, a singular and alarming accident occurred at Pocklington, which might have had a tragic sequel. A three horse waggon, belonging to Mr. W. Gibson, of Thornton, had been laden with oil cake in the railway station yard, and the driver, George Lowther, was just about to mount the saddle horse when the front animal became frightened and all three horses galloped out of the yard and made for the railway gates at the end of the station, the driver pluckily sticking to the reins.

At the very moment the horse plunged into the gates the 3-35 pm express train from York drew up, with the result that they caught one of the gates and smashed it to atoms. Lowther just relinquished the reins in time, or he must surely have been jammed into the moving train, and sufffered a cruel fate. Rebounding from the impact the distracted horses careered madly into the pallisading, surmounting a garden wall of Mr. Coverdale's residence, breaking several railings and displacing the brickwork. Meanwhile help was forthcoming, and the horses were unyoked, and the front animal which was terribly wounded, bleeding profusely, taken to the New Red Lion stables, where Mr. Jebson was soon in attendance. He found that the oven bone was completely shattered and the rear hip was severely injured. Whether it recovers remains to be seen. Returning to the engine, it fortunately kept the METALS, and there were several passengers in the train who did not know, until afterwards, that an accident had occurred. The only damage sustained by the engine was a displaced spring. Lord Herries happened to be in the train and his carriage was bespattered with blood, and as soon as the accident occurred he enquired as to whether anybody had been hurt. It is stated as a curious, not as a comical coincidence, that the train from Hull, about the same time, killed a HEN just before entering Pocklington Station.

May, 1896

THE CYCLE FEVER – POCKLINGTON

It has been pointed out the danger occasioned by TRI CYCLISTS careering about the streets endangering life and limb. It was thought precautionary measures should be taken. Also reference has been made to the practice of cyclists learning to ride on a Sunday and the din they make in the streets, howling and shouting.

May, 1896

COMMERCIAL TRAVELLER IN PERIL AT FANGFOSS

On Thursday afternoon a commercial traveller from York was driving near Fangfoss and took his horse for a drink at the pond at the road end. Thinking it was a shallow, shelving declivity, he drove in without hesitation, and before he knew where he was, the horse was struggling in deep water. For a time matters looked very serious, but ultimately help was forthcoming and by means of ropes, etc., man and horse were saved from a dangerous predicament.

June, 1896

PAPER CHASE ON CYCLES

On Monday evening a novel paper chase took place, which created great interest and fun. The "hares" were Miss Fairweather and the Reverend J. Bridges of Goodmanham, and they were sent off at 5 pm on the road to Market Weighton. The "hounds", numbering some 18, comprising 6 or 7 ladies, started on the chase some 10 minutes after and followed their quarries to Hayton, through Nunburnholme, and on to Warter. The scent led on to Kilnwick and then to Pocklington, from where the hounds made back to Goodmanham, where they arrived after a splendid sprint. The "hounds" were outpaced and never caught sight of their "victims". Only 1 lady rider survived to tell the tale, the heroine being Miss I. Anson, a visitor of Goodmanham Rectory. The chase was voted a great success and was thoroughly enjoyed by all who participated, and probably this is only the trial of v ha will become a very diverting and popular pastime.

June, 1896

STARTLING STREET INCIDENT AT POCKLINGTON

On Monday, a horse and four wheeled rulley, containing planks for the new houses on Barmby Road, was being driven from the Station Yard, Pocklington, when the horse took fright in Railway Street and galloped off at a furious pace. A youth named Albert Tayleure was riding on top of the planks, which, when they lost their equilibrium, shot him up into the air as from a catapult, and he fell on his knees on the ground with an ugly thud. When the horse got to Browns Corner, it upset a heap of boxes, and eventually dashed into the side-windows, smashing the glass and damaging one of the supports. It then collided with the donkey and cart belonging to Mr. Cockerill of Barmby Moor, and was brought to a standstill. The driver, Leonard Richardson, pluckily stuck to his reins and averted further mishap, otherwise the consequences might have been serious.

June, 1896

A REAPER OVERTURNED AT BURNBY

On Monday morning, about 6 am, two horses belonging to Mr. Dobson of Burnby, were drawing a REAPER belonging to Mr. Wyrill, in a field at Burnby, when one of the horses began to kick and got his feet over the pole. This frightened the other horse and both horses galloped into a corner of the field and turned the reaper into a gutter, smashing the machine and giving the horses a severe fright. Mr. Wyrill's son, William, was driving at the time the accident occurred and had a wonderful escape from injury, the reins breaking and the young man falling backwards way over.

July, 1896

RUNAWAY HORSE AT POCKLINGTON

On Wednesday, a carter named John Henry BUTTLE, of Beckside, Pocklington, was yoking a horse and had got all the harness adjusted, with the exception of the kicking straps, when the horse bolted, with Buttle in pursuit. It ran down New Street, where Mr. G. B. Wilberforce, bank manager, had a narrow escape of being knocked down, and the animal turned down Burnby Lane. Meanwhile, Buttle who had held gamely to the reins, tried hard to bring the horse up, and in doing so unfortunately was jammed between the cart and a lamp post situate near the flower show field, and received very severe injuries.

September, 1896

SERIOUS ACCIDENT AT THE WHITE MILLS, POCKLINGTON

On Thursday, as Mr. J. Thirsk (head of the firm of Thirsk & Sons, White Mills, Pocklington) was superintending the unloading of some waggons which had come up to the Mill by the newly made railway siding, when he by some means or other, got jammed between a wall and one of the waggons, sustaining a serious bruise on the upper part of the chest. Fortunately he fell onto the ground or else the consequences could have proved fatal. Now under the care of the local doctor, he is progressing favourably.

September, 1896

West Green as seen from White Mills, Pocklington

"STRAYING ON THE HIGHWAY" – a letter
– Complaint from a BARMBY MOOR resident.

Dear Sir,

I have a grievance to ventilate and would crave a space in your valuable paper. For sometime now I have looked upon it as a great inconvenience, as well as a palpable danger, to those persons riding, or driving, or cycling, that so many animals of various species are allowed to stray on the highways. The nuisance appears to grow, and that no place is it greater than at Barmby Moor. I believe that according to law, no live animal is allowed to stray on the highway, and what with a NUISANCE INSPECTOR and Parish Councillors, one would have thought the problem would have been remedied. I have been told there is a doubt about there being a Parish Council, and if that body is such a nonentity as that implies, it accounts for the nuisance still being allowed. I suppose I have passed over the bridge for 9 years now but never have I seen the nuisance so bad as at present.

Your truly,
A RESIDENT

October, 1896

MOTOR CAR AT HULL

A motor car has been tried at Hull and in all probabilty motor power will also be applied to the 4 fire engines belonging to the North Eastern Railway Company.

November, 1896

SHOCKING FATALITY AT WAPLINGTON
– CHILDS LIFE CRUSHED OUT

On Wednesday, at Waplington, at 3.30 pm, a child, 3 years of age, named John Albert Collins, whose father is bailiff at the Low farm, was playing in the stack-yard. There was a loose gate leaning against a wall, and to the gate was attached some strings. It is believed that the little boy was playing with the string, and by this means caused the gate to fall on top of him. Death was almost instantaneous. Dr. Angus Fairweather said that death resulted from the fracture of the spine in the region of the neck and the verdict was recorded in accordance with the medical evidence. The parents were exonerated from all blame in the sad accident.

November, 1896

LADY CYCLIST ON THE FOOTPATH – POCKLINGTON

The Council Foreman reported to the Surveyor that on Wednesday evening just at dusk, he found a Pocklington lady riding a bicycle on the West Green. He informed her that it was illegal and that he would have to report the matter. She then went on the high road for a few yards but afterwards resumed riding on the footpath. As he had already had instructions from the Council to proceed against persons for these offences, he proposed to take out a summons against the lady in question.

December, 1896

COLLISION NEAR HAYTON

On Tuesday evening a collision occurred near Hayton between a trap, containing Mr. Theakstone of Hayton, Mr. Greig of Pocklington, and a wagonette conveying a team of football players journeying from Pocklington. The night was dark and stormy, and we understand that neither of the conveyances had lights. The result of the impact was that one of the wagonette horses, which belonged to Mr. Swales of Market Weighton, was killed, whilst some of the occupants of the conveyance were severely shaken, and minor damage was done.

March, 1897

A ROOSHING PONIES CANTER

George Wincup of Shipton, was charged with driving a vehicle at a furious pace. Police Constable Smith said that on the date in question he was on duty at THORPE LE STREET and defendant drove along the York road at a gallop of 18 miles per hour, and a cyclist riding alongside fell over. He held up his hand for defendant to stop but he only slackened speed slightly, he afterwards saw defendant at Shipton and defendant said "When the old b..... gets started I cannot stop it". Defendant said his "ROOSHING PONY" could not canter more than 7 miles per hour as to 18 miles per hour "There is not SIKE a thing WAD happen". A witness named J. Johnson said defendant was driving at a gallop and simply trotted on when Constable held up his hand to stop him. Fined 10/- and costs.

June, 1897

BOY KILLED BY AN ENGINE – HULL

A terrible fatality occurred at DAIRYCOATES yesterday. An engine cleaner named Arthur Dick, aged 15, was picking up a letter which had been thrown from

Beverley Road, Hull

Market Weighton Station

a passing engine, when he was knocked down by another engine which came unnoticed from the other direction.

The poor lad was badly injured and Dr. Stone of HESSLE Road was promptly brought to his aid. Dick breathed his last before the arrival of the doctor.

June, 1897

LARGE LOAD AT WITHERNSEA

The arrival last Tuesday in the shape of a boiler, weight 15 tons, for the "WHITCOAT, WITHERNSEA BRICK AND TILE WORKS", caused no little excitement on its removal from the station to its destination by the powerful steam traction engine belonging to Mr. George Dales, of WELWICK.

June, 1897

BEVERLEY ROAD TRANSPORT

Forty years ago there was one omnibus on the Beverley Road, running from Rose Cottage to Hull at a fare of 3d. Now there are 83 wagonettes doing a very good business with penny rides, in addition to the trams.

July, 1897

HULL TO GOOLE TRIPPERS

The steamer "HER MAJESTY" yesterday brought a boatfull of trippers from Hull, arriving at Goole at 5.30 pm and returning at 7 pm. The ride along the river was exceedingly pleasant and is much preferred to the Humber, and the trip to Grimsby. There is more to be seen along the banks of the OUSE for one thing.

July, 1897

RAIL IMPORTANCE – DRIFFIELD

Driffield is now more than ever a place of importance on account of its railway facilities and as a junction. A Driffielder can now go to London, spend 4 hours there, and be home again almost in the space of 12 hours.

On Saturday 8 or 9 excursions rattle through the station at Driffield, from South and West Yorkshire, several of them being in duplicate. The Market Weighton and Driffield line is made use of to an amazing extent for mineral traffic and "foreign" passenger trains.

July, 1897

COLLIDED WITH A LAMP POST – HULL

William Parkinson of Richmond Terrace, Hull, a rulleyman in the employment of the North Eastern Railway Company, was in charge of his rulley in English Street, when the horse bolted into Kingston Street, where it collided with a lamp post.

The lamp post was slightly bent to one side, and the gas burner knocked off. Thankfully there were no real injuries.

July, 1897

Chapter IV

LIFE AT THE WORKHOUSE
– POVERTY

OVERCROWDING WORKHOUSES IN YORKSHIRE

At the meeting of the DRIFFIELD Board of Guardians on Thursday, a letter was read from the Halifax Board of Guardians, stating that their workhouse was overcrowded and asking if the Driffield authorities would be willing to take into their care 100 paupers – in response to the Chairman the Master said there was no accommodation at Driffield. There was double the number of men in the day room that there ought to be – it was decided not to entertain the application.

January, 1885

HULL BOARD OF GUARDIANS

There are some pitiable cases in Hull, where the children attending the Board Schools, go to school without having tasted breakfast. One case in particular we have heard of where a little boy told the Headmaster of one of the Hull schools that he had never had breakfast, and only had dinner when he received a ticket from the Schoolchildren Hope Society.

February, 1895

PROVIDING FOR HUNGRY SCHOOLCHILDREN

At an executive meeting of the HULL SCHOOLCHILDREN HOPE SOCIETY, held at the town hall on Wednesday, the Chairman said that since the last meeting there had been issued 10,655 tickets, at a cost of £47 10s. The weather had not improved and the distress had not diminished.

There was as great – indeed in some cases – greater need for help as there was four months ago. He hoped the present appeal would be largely responded to by the Public. Mr. Grant said that tickets were placed in the hands of the teachers in each department of the elementary schools and the teachers gave the tickets to the needy children. The Society had provided meals at 18 different centres. Each meal averaged 1d per head (penny farthing). The tickets issued this season numbered 28,416. At one school children were to be seen without boots, their feet being wrapped in rags. Mr. Tewell said that in the Chapman Street School there were about 23 children who did not know what it was to have breakfast, and the only meals they got were those provided by the Society.

The Chairman said that the balance in the bank now stood at £145 4s 3d. Mr. Grant stated that unless they received other funds the operation of the Society would have to cease in 3 weeks time. It was decided to provide £55 for the next 2 weeks.

February, 1895

Thirty four degrees of frost was recorded at Cottingham on 9th February, 1895

HUNGER – HULL

An instance of hunger and poverty was witnessed in Brooke Street on Tuesday afternoon, which would have softened the hardest hearts. A little fellow, thinly clad, and with shoeless feet, and a look of starvation on his pinched face, was hurrying along, biting away at a piece of soda stone. A passerby observed the distress of the youngster and interrogated him about his troubles. As tears rolled down the pale cheeks of the little hungry one, he informed the inquirer that he had had no food since Monday morning and so he had tried to eat the soda stone. The questioner was so touched by such a pathetic instance of suffering that he was quite overcome and he took the boy to a coffee house and provided him with a substantial meal.

February, 1895

SOUP KITCHEN – HULL

At the JUBILEE PRIMITIVE METHODIST CHAPEL, Spring Bank, Hull, there was given away again about 100 quarts of soup and about 100 loaves of bread. This is the third week bread and soup have been given and been distributed.

March, 1895

ASKING FOR A WIFE

The members of the Hull Board of Guardians stared at each other in blank astonishment, which gave way to loud laughter, when the Governor announced at the weekly meeting of a singular application he had received. It reads as follows:-

"I want to know if I can get a young woman out of the Workhouse to get married to". The Governor did not mention the name of this indiscrimitive lovesick applicant, but said he was on board a smack at sea. He had the smack's name and number. The applicant kindly asked if they would communicate with him at sea. Someone present suggested that one of the female inmates should be sent out to him to meet his requirements.

March, 1895

CHRISTMAS DAY AT THE WORKHOUSE – POCKLINGTON

The inmates of the "Big House" are, as usual, to have their share of Christmas Fare, and plum pudding and roast beef will come in for a good share of attention on Christmas Day. The Master and Matron have spared no pains to make the interior brighter and more attractive, and with evergreens kindly supplied by Major General Duncombe, they have had plenty of material to work upon. A very well laden Christmas tree will bring joy to the youngsters, and the day that brings to them absolute possession will minister untold delight to their little hearts.

December, 1895

AUDICIOUS BURGLARY AT POCKLINGTON WORKHOUSE
THE DEPREDATOR SCOT FREE –

In the early hours of Saturday last, the boardroom of the Pocklington Workhouse was burglariously entered and rifled. The Master and Matron retired to rest at about eleven o'clock, on the previous night, and before going upstairs, they made sure, as usual, that all was secure, at least as secure as lock and bolt could make them. Next morning, the Master, Mr. Sargent, was up betimes, and was not long in discovering that some uninfected guest had been on the premises. The normal serenity of the boardroom had been rudely disturbed and the Master found himself minus an overcoat, coat and vest, whilst the sacriligious hand had also been laid upon the missionary box. The burglar had then found his way to the men's bedroom, and evidently taken a fancy to a pair of boots, in a chamber for once wanted they were decidely "Gone". A cupboard in the boardroom had claimed the unsolicited attention of the visitor for then he had made short work of a cake that had been stored away. Fortunately, however, some silver plated goods in the same recepticle had been left severely alone. It is shrewdly supposed that a former inmate is the culprit, and sufficient is known to lead to identification should a chance offer. Entrance had been effected by the catch of one of the boardroom windows having been pushed back by a knife. Curious places have been rifled before at curious times, and under curious circumstance, but this is our first acquaintance with BILL SYKES on business bent in a workhouse.

January, 1896

INSPECTION OF THE WORKHOUSE – POCKLINGTON

Mr Robson read the report of Dr. Needham, visiting Commissioner of LUNACY, which stated that he had inspected the house on the 30th August last. He found the same 3 men and 6 women who had previously been seen by his colleagues were the only classed imbeciles in the Workhouse on that date. One man was in the infirmary and the others were in the body of the House. All were neatly dressed and their appearances gave him a favourable impression of their care. Everything was clean, and their dietary care appeared to be adequate. Some of the women worked, and all have considerable liberty within the Workhouse. The beds and bedding were very clean. A new laundry and other buildings having been completed and a new bathroom was in the course of erection.

September, 1896

Pocklington Union Workhouse

SAD DEATH OF A PAUPER - CHOKED AT DINNER – POCKLINGTON

Yesterday, Coroner Wood held an inquest at the Pocklington Workhouse on the body of Robert Turner, an inmate, aged 75 years, who choked on Wednesday afternoon whilst partaking of his dinner. Thomas Turner, labourer of George Street, said the deceased who was his brother, had been a labourer all his life. Edward ALLIBONE, a pauper inmate, said deceased was having his dinner on Wednesday along with the other 11 inmates of the day room at the hospital. Bacon and potatoes were the fayre for the dinner, the bacon being boiled and fairly cut. The attention of witness was called to deceased by his choking. He succeeded in getting two pieces, about 1 inch square, out of his mouth. Deceased continued to be black in the face, and witness sent for Master and Matron, who came at once. Witness said witness and the Master tried to extract what appeared to be another piece of food from his throat, but could not do so, deceased died within a few minutes. Deceased was very weak and aged, he had been warned not to eat too fast. Dr. Angus Fairweather said that he had been called to see the deceased on Wednesday, and found him on the floor, he had just expired. He appeared to have died from choking. The jury returned a verdict of death from accidental choking, and made an almost unanimous declaration that in future the Guardians employ a trained nurse at the Workhouse. This did not imply the slightest reflection on the means to save the poor fellow as everything possible was done to rescue him.

October, 1896

POCKLINGTON BOARD OF GUARDIANS

– a matter for the Committee.

The Master, Mr Sargent, reported the general servant, or by common courtesy, the Assistant Matron, for alleged violent temper and unruliness, and she submitted her resignation by letter, whereupon she was brought upon before the Board and asked to explain her conduct. She denied the impingement, and said she had been put upon by her superiors. The Master and Matron entirely repudiated any suggestion of harsh treatment, and said they had always tried to make the servant as comfortable as possible. The matter was fully discussed and decided upon by the Committee.

December, 1896

REFUSAL TO WORK

Last Saturday two men named Henry Collinson and Thomas White were sent to prison for 14 days, for refusing to do their task work at the Pocklington Work House.

January, 1897

RICH INMATE – DRIFFIELD

On an inmate at the Driffield Workhouse during a search recently, it was found that he had on him £54 15s 6d and a bank book in his possession.

The man has told the Chairman of the Board of Guardians that he was entirely comfortable in his quarters, but he wanted a shilling or two in his pocket, and to wear the Workhouse clothes, because he looked so singular in his own clothes.

June, 1897

Chapter V

CRIMES

ABSCONDING FARM SERVANTS
– Exemplary sentences by the Pocklington Magistrates.

At the Pocklington Police Courts on Saturday, a farm servant, named William Daniells, lately with Mr. E. R. Templeton, a farmer of Hayton, was ordered to pay 15/- and 3/- costs for illegally quitting his master's service. He being 3 days at "his place". Defendant left without making any complaint.

– Joseph Potter, farm servant, on a similar conviction of absconding from the service of Mr. Jonathon Beale of Sutton on Derwent was ordered to pay £2 compensation and costs of 4s-6d.

– Robert Whitehead also a farm servant, recently with Mr. Robert Copeland, farmer of Storwood, was ordered to pay £1-10s and costs of 3/- for absconding. He said he had no cause for leaving except that he could not settle.

January, 1895

A HULL WOMAN IN TROUBLE AT GOOLE
Yesterday morning, at the Goole Police Court, Mary Ann Walden, who stated that she had come from Hull, was charged with stealing the sum of 1s in silver, the property of Mr. Hopley, by means of a trick known as "RINGING THE CHANGES". The complainant, James Hopley, fruiterer, of Aire Street, said that the prisoner came in to his shop on the 23rd inst. and asked for a lemon. She gave him a shilling in payment, and he handed her 11d in change. She then said she wanted a penny one, but complainant had none, and handed back the shilling. She replied that she would take 2 for 1d which he gave her, and asked for his money. She said she had already given him a shilling.

P.C. Quigley proved apprehending the prisoner, who was further charged with stealing another shilling from Messrs. Moss and Son, grocers of Ouse Street, by similar means. Henry Moss gave evidence, and the prisoner pleaded guilty. The Bench remarked that she had previously been up for the same thing, and committed her to prison for 1 month with hard labour.

January, 1895

ATTEMPTED SUICIDE AT SNAITH
At Police Court on Wednesday, before Mayor Eden and Mr. J. Norwood, William Roberts of Whitley, farmer, was charged with attempting to take his life at his residence at Whitley, on the day previous. P.S. Huntingdon stated that he found the prisoner tied by his garters tightly round the neck of his bedstead. After releasing him he charged him, when he replied "It is nonsense". The prisoner who had been drinking heavily of late asked the bench to give him another chance. However it was stated that only recently he had tried to drown himself by jumping into the AIRE and CALDER canal but was rescued. It was ultimately decided to remand the prisoner for 8 days.

January, 1895

DRINKING AND GAMBLING IN AN OUTHOUSE – HULL

James Revell, labourer, was charged on remand, at the Hull Police Court yesterday with stealing a small quantity of coal, valued at 4d., from the Alexandra Dock on the 25th January the property of the Hull and Barnsley Railway company. Prisoner pleaded guilty, and said there was no fire in his house – he was given a good character by a Hull and Barnsley employee – P.C. Onions of the Hull and Barnsley Police, said that the prisoner and other men stole coal, and took it to an outhouse, where they went at night spending their time drinking and gambling. Prisoner said he had never been there in his life. Prisoner was fined 10s 6d.

February, 1895

TRAVELLING WITHOUT A TICKET

At the Howden Petty Sessions, William Buller, a bookmaker, and farmer of Eastrington, was charged with travelling on a North Eastern Railway without having previously paid his fare, and with intent to defraud the said railway company.

Inspector Strafford of the North Eastern Railway Companies Police had the case in hand. It appears that on the 10th December, the defendant had been noticed by the ticket collector at Selby to arrive by the 12.45 train from Hull, and he arrived at Eastrington by the 3.15 from Selby. He there said he got in at Howden and offered 1s to the Clerk. It was, however, shown that he did not get into Howden with the train.

Mr. Douglas, from the Solicitors office of the Company, prosecuted. The Inspector afterwards visited Mr. Buller at his house in Eastrington, where the offence was admitted and begged of the Inspector to get the Company not to prosecute. Mrs. Buller, his wife, appeared and said that her husband was unable to attend, having been kicked by a horse. The Bench considered the case fully proved, and inflicted a penalty of £2 and costs in all of £3-8s.

February, 1895

FIGHTING ON THE WESTWOOD

Two labourers named Rountree Best and Richard Bristol, who were staying at Beverley on Saturday, quarrelled. This resulted in paying a visit to the Westwood, where P.C. Wood found them fighting, Best without his shirt on. They were parted, and the end was that proceedings were taken against them for being drunk and disorderly. Neither appeared at the Police Court on Monday, and the Justices made an order for 14 days imprisonment against each man.

March, 1895

"STROLLING ROUND THE TOWN"

On Saturday, at Pocklington Police Court, four young men, named Leonard Richardson, John Durkin, Richard Skelton, and Thomas Harrison, all of Pocklington were charged with being drunk and disorderly in the Market Place on 17th December, 1894. Richardson was charged with assaulting Frank Rippon, who was engaged in putting out the street lamps. Defendants denied being drunk and submitted that they were out CAROL practising for Christmas – Richardson was fined 15/- and the others 13/-.

January, 1895

New Pavement, Pocklington. The 3 terraced buildings on the right have long since been demolished. The resulting area is now the Churchyard and the main gates to the Church

DRUNK DRIVING AT MARKET WEIGHTON

Edmund Johnson of Market Weighton was on Wednesday fined 13/-, including costs, at Market Weighton Court, for being drunk in charge of a horse and cart.

March, 1895

SEATON ROSS PARENTS SUMMONED

On Wednesday, at the Weighton Police Court, Mrs. Jane Hutchinson of Seaton Ross was fined 1/- for not sending her child regularly to school. A similar charge against John Ridsdale was adjourned, the child being said to suffer from fainting fits.

March, 1895

UNLAWFUL POSSESSION OF ROOKES – BEVERLEY

Joseph Henry G, George S, George G, young men living in Dog and Duck Lane, Beverley, were summoned before the East Riding Justices at Beverley, last Saturday, charged under the Wild Birds Protection Act, with having a number of Rookes in their possession at Walkington Goldwalls on the 10th instant. G. did not appear, the other two defendants pleaded guilty, – Sergeant Parker, who stated the facts of the case, said he met the defendants at about half past four in the morning with a number of Rookes in their possession. The defendants were reprimanded and discharged on paying the costs.

June, 1895

EAST RIDING CRIME

It is gratifying to note that crime in the East Riding is on the decrease. The number of persons committed to Hull Prison from the East Riding for quarter ending 31st March, 1894, was 75 whereas for the quarter just ended, the number was 62.

April, 1895

ATTEMPTED SUICIDE NEAR BEVERLEY

A woman about 30 years of age, named Emily Cussens, was charged before the East Ridings Magistrate, on Saturday, with attempting to commit suicide by walking into the River Hull. As she had been in prison for several days, the bench dismissed the case, on the understanding that her friends, who were in Court, would look after her.

June, 1895

A BEGGING CASE

At the Market Weighton Police Court, on Wednesday, before the Reverend R. G. Willis, three young men, named John Connelly, Francis Flynn, and Joseph Brannen, were charged with begging at the Reformatory School. The prisoners, only came out of jail on the 8th for a like offence. The Reverend P. Castellano said they were continually begging. On 24th May last, he gave to Connelly and Flynn a pedlars certificate and goods to the value of 10s 6d each, but they were too idle to hawk them. The prisoners were now sentenced to one months hard labour. When they heard their sentence, they asked the Chairman to give them 5 weeks.

June, 1895

CHILD ASSAULTED AT BARMBY MOOR

At a special sitting at the Pocklington Police Court on Tuesday, a Barmby Moor labourer, named John D....., was charged on remand with criminally assaulting his own daughter, named Mary Ellen, aged 7. The prosecution instituted by the Society for the Prevention of Cruelty to Children, was tersely outlined to the court before calling the witnesses. The evidence was too revolting for publication. Suffice to say that Dr. Leadman deposed to the fact that the child had undoubtedly been outraged. The prisoner was committed for trial at the forthcoming Assizes, bail being offered, prisoner in £20 and two sureties of £10 each. Later in the day, the bail was not forthcoming and prisoner was conveyed to York Castle.

The ALLEGED assault at Barmby Moor on Wednesday at the York Assizes. John D., labourer, was indicted for criminally assaulting his daughter, Mary Ellen. After the evidence of the prosecution, the jury, after a short retirement, found prisoner not guilty and he was discharged.

June, 1895

AN ALLEGED DASTARDLY ASSAULT AT SHIPTON

On Wednesday afternoon, a one armed man, named James Kelly, of no fixed abode, but who is well known about the Howden District, was walking through Shipton, when he saw a butchers cart and asked the driver for a "PENNORTH" of liver, and the driver in reply said he would give him "TWO PENNORTH" with which it is alleged he took a kick at him, and was helped by two other men. All three set on him in this shameful manner until a gentleman, on seeing the row, went to the man's assistance. Kelly was fearfully cut and bruised and had lost a great quantity of blood. He went to Market Weighton and laid information at the Police Station, and summonses have been granted.

September, 1895

A MAD ACT AT MARKET WEIGHTON
– FIERY CORN WAGGON

On Thursday afternoon at about 4.30 pm, a waggon belonging to Mr. Brough, of Market Weighton, and laden with Barley, was being driven down Sweep Lane, Market Weighton. A boy named Sherwood ran behind the waggon, struck a match, and set fire to the corn at the back part of the waggon. Almost immediately the fire spread all over the load. The driver had the presence of mind to get the horses out of the waggon, and help arriving immediately, the fire was extinguished, but not before both corn and waggon had been partially destroyed.

September, 1895

A YAPHAM MAN DRUNK ON HORSEBACK

At Pocklington, on Saturday, Thomas King of Yapham, for being drunk whilst on horseback, was fined £1 and costs of 3s. 6d. Superintendent Rawlings saw the defendant riding from Pocklington very drunk and apparently in great danger of falling off his horse. Police Constable Ridsdill found defendant on the roadside going to Yapham. He and another man had to carry defendant to the police station.

September, 1895

A TIMBER MERCHANTS DRIVE THROUGH MELBOURNE

At Pocklington Police Court on Saturday, John Whitelock, timber merchant, was charged with being drunk in charge of a horse and trap at Melbourne on the 17th September. Police Constable Harrison said that at about 6-15 he saw the defendant in charge of a horse and trap at Melbourne. Defendant was very drunk and driving recklessly in the village. He drove on the footpath, and nearly upset the trap. Witness came on to him near the Cross Keys Hotel. Defendant was so drunk that he could not make anything of him. Witness got into the trap, and drove the defendant towards Pocklington. He had considerable difficulty in getting him to the Police Station. Police Constable Nicholson on duty at the Police Station, corroborated, and stated that the defendant used very abusive language and refused for a time to give his name and address. Defendant, who denied the offence, was fined £1 and costs of 3s.

September, 1895

CAPITAL TOO FAR – MELBOURNE

Alfred Manning, for illegally quitting the service of Thomas Whitfield, a farmer, of Melbourne, was ordered to pay £2 compensation and 3/- costs. Defendant was hired on the 15th January for £20-10s to Martinmas, as foreman waggoner. He came into service on the 18th January, and left on the 21st. On the 21st the defendant was delivering potatoes to the Pocklington Station, and returned late. His master complained and defendant offered his "fest" 5/- back again, remarking that it was too far to Pocklington in "half a day". The "fest" (FEST) was refused, and the defendant was ordered to finish his work for the day. He left the same night.

January, 1896

EXCITING CHASE ON HORSEBACK
– CLEVER POLICE CAPTURE

Sergeant Maw, of Pocklington, had a lively experience on Wednesday night, when he rode some 6 miles in pursuit of a chimney sweep, from MALTON named J. W. Swales, whom he eventually captured.

On Wednesday night at almost 6 pm information was conveyed to the police station that the man Swales had been at the WELLINGTON OAK INN, at RIVERHEAD, and after refusing to quit the premises he had assaulted the Landlord's nephew, Albert Harrison. It was further stated that Swales had broken several windows and some trellis work with his machine sticks. On receipt of the information Sergeant Maw promptly secured a mount and, not withstanding the fact that this man had got some 3 miles start, the Sergeant by dint of inquiries and hard riding, came upon with Swales in the vicinity of HARSWELL, and brought him back to Pocklington, arriving at the Police Station at about 10 pm after an exciting chase.

May, 1896

TRIED THREE TIMES

County Court cases, said his Honour at Pocklington, on Tuesday, are tried three times. Once before the Court sat, Once at the Court, and Once after.

June, 1896

EAST RIDING CRIME FIGURES

At the quarterly meeting of the East Riding Standing Joint Committee, at which Alderman Calverley Rudston and Councillor H. Syd. Powell represented Pocklington District, the Chief Constable reported that during the past quarter, 565 persons had been taken before the Justices, of the East Riding, of whom 6 were committed for trial, 451 summarly convicted, and 103 discharged. These figures represented a decrease. Six fires had occurred, doing damage to the amount of £4713, of which only £50 was not covered by insurance.

The Committee recommended that the number of Constables at Bridlington should be increased by 2 or 3 men. Twelve bicycles had been ordered for use at the different Police Stations at £12-16s-0d each.

July, 1896

FIRING RIFLES – POCKLINGTON

Charged under the PUBLIC CLAUSES ACT V12, discharging firearms in the public street. On being charged, defendant admitted the offence. John Wreggitt, a roadman in the employ of the Urban Council, stated that on the 1st July, at about half past eight in the night, he had been standing at the junction of Railway Street and REGENT STREET, when he had heard the report of firearms, ten or twelve shots having been fired. It appears the Volunteers were returning from drill, and when they passed him he noticed the defendant amongst them. Witness then saw defendant raise his rifle to his shoulder and discharge it. Mr. Summerson, for the Prosecution, pointed out that defendant had rendered himself liable to a penalty of £2 and the offence was a very serious one, which, if not stopped, might cause a good deal of harm. Defendant said he fired without any bad intention, and he was very sorry for the offence. The Bench said as it was the first case of the kind, a fine of 2s 6d and costs of 4s would be inflicted.

August, 1896

BEGGING AT WARTER PRIORY

On Wednesday two tramps named Boyle and Bradley, were convicted before Councillor Grant for begging at Warter Priory and were sent to York Castle for 14 days.

August, 1896

NO LIGHTS – HAYTON

Fred Bell of NEWPORT, was charged with riding on the road to HAYTC.. without a lamp. Police Constable Harris said that on the 20th July, at about half past twelve at midnight, he accosted the defendant on his machine which was without lamps. Defendant said he had lit up his lamp at Pocklington, and it must have gone out and he had no more MATCHES. The Bench fined him 2s 6d and costs of 3s.

August, 1896

WATERED WHISKY – WILBERFOSS

Robert Walker, landlord of the Blacksmiths Arms, WILBERFOSS, was charged with selling adulterated whisky on the 21st August. Superintendant Rawlings purchased the whisky for analysis. The certificate of Mr. Baines of Hull gave 7.5% of added water. Fined 5s.

September, 1896

OBSTRUCTION CASE
– A Weighton grocer fined.

Elizabeth Gullick, a Market Weighton grocer and provisions dealer, in High Street, was charged with obstructing the footpath by placing thereon 2 barrels, 19 boxes, and 1 sack bag of wheat, 2 sack bags of meal, and a sack barrow. Inspector Clarkson said that on the 17th September, he found the articles ennumerated above on the footpath in front of the defendant's shop, and they remained there from 9.30 to 12.25, when the Railway Rulleyman took them away. During the interval he saw several persons, who were walking on the footpath, turn aside because of these obstructions. He went inside and informed Mr. Gullick, the defendant's son, that he should report the case. It was stated that it was the custom of local tradesmen to put their empties on the footpath ready for removal by the North Eastern Railway Company and that is what had been done by the case in question. The Magistrates Clerk pointed out that the Act under which proceedings had been taken out had been in force for 60 years. The Magistrate said they must deal with the case according to law, and the defendant would be fined 1/- and costs.

October, 1896

A WIDOW AGED - AND DRUNK – POCKLINGTON

Last Saturday at Pocklington, before Councillor Thomas Grant, a widow aged 68, named Anna STYAN, was fined 10/- and costs, or 14 days, for being drunk at Pocklington. She went to York Castle for 14 days.

October, 1896

IMPUDENT THEFT AT MARKET WEIGHTON

At Market Weighton on Thursday, John Jackson, a tramp, was sentenced to prison for 7 days for stealing a loaf of bread, the property of Mrs. Barbara Julian. It appeared the prisoner had gone into the shop and ordered some bacon and bread and eventually ate the bread without paying for it. He was brought to book by Mr. Julian and became insolent hence these proceedings.

October, 1896

BRUTAL ASSAULT IN A POTATO FIELD

Thomas Harrison of Pocklington, was charged with assaulting Elizabeth Harrison, on the 8th October. Complainant said they were working in a potato field at Waplington, when the defendant said she was not doing as much as he was and she replied that she thought she was. He then said "No you are not you ...... thing" and he hit her across the face knocking her down. He afterwards knocked her down again. Defendant was fined 10/- and 6s 6d costs.

November, 1896

STEALING DRYING CLOTHES AT HOLME

At a special meeting of the Market Weighton Police Court, two youthful tramps named Michael Walch and Joseph Conray, were sent to prison for 7 days for stealing a couple of coloured handkerchiefs, the property of Mr. William Watson of Holme upon Spalding Moor. The articles in question had been placed upon a hedge near the house to dry, and prisoners were observed to hook them off. They were apprehended by Police Constable Nicholson.

January, 1897

A CASE FROM HAYTON

A lad named Alfred Frear, 15, sued Mr. Templeman, farmer from Hayton, for wages not produced. He said he went to defendants on October 6th, 1896, and was in his service 11 weeks. He had to drive the cows to and from milking twice a day, and he walked about 8 miles a day. Defendant once gave half a crown but no wage was fixed and he felt 3/- per week was fair remuneration. His Honour gave judgement to the plaintiff for £1 5s 6d.

April, 1897

AN OLD WOMAN'S PLEA – HULL

An old woman pleaded for mercy yesterday at the Hull Sessions. She had already suffered 15 years penal servitude – 8 years for stealing a shawl, and 7 years for taking a pair of boots – and even Council for the prosecution admitted that they were terribly severe sentences for such paltry crimes.

Mr. Forbes pitied the unfortunate woman and sentenced her to 7 days. The prisoner who could scarcely comprehend the judge's remarks turned to a warder and inquired "7 years did he say?" When she learned the sentence she was overjoyed beyond expression.

July, 1897

AFRAID OF HIS WIFE – HULL

A man named Barratt was summoned at the Hull Police Court, on Tuesday, for deserting his wife – defendant said he had left her because he was afraid of her. Once she had thrown a bucket of water over him – a separation order of 3s 6d per week was made.

July, 1897

Chapter VI

FIRE

FIRE AT MR. GRANTS WAREHOUSE
(FORMERLY THE VICTORIA HALL, AND LATTERLY
R. M. ENGLISH'S MILL, DEMOLISHED LATE 1989)

The Mill.

Lay-out. The mill consisted of 2 original Georgian mill buildings connected at the front and rear by matching centre span walls. These fake walls were constructed in 1897.

Prior to 1897 plan view of the mill was in the shape of a 'U' – the 2 outer buildings connected at the rear by a narrow low passage. This plan form can be seen on the 1844 and 1855 maps of Pocklington by William Watson.

History. William Scorborough, yeoman, and Christopher Moore, grocer, both of Pocklington ordered 100,000 bricks to be made from clay from the Ings of Pocklington. The brickmaker was a Robert Pickerings of York. This was in 1684.

It is believed that the right hand building of the mill was constructed in the early 1700's. This is yet to be verified. It is estimated that this building required about 70,000 bricks. The roof timbers that spanned the walls were 'roughly cleaned' up tree trunks laid across the walls. It is also believed that the building was named after its use and that was "Oak House".

By 1685 there were at least 3 tanners in Pocklington, John Radcliffe, John Bielby

Mr Grant's Warehouse, formerly the Victoria Hall, Chapmangate, Pocklington. Note the fire blackened frontage from the fire of 1896. Demolished late 1989

and his father Robert. From the records of their inventories they clearly were among the wealthiest families in Pocklington.

By 1730 it is know that a tanyard was in operation on the land between Chapmangate and Union Street, alongside the present mill site. It is probable that one of the above families operated the tanyard.

During the years between 1776 and 1833 the tanyard was owned by the Wilson family.

On it sale in 1833 the Union Street side of the tanyard was described thus:-

"A Capital Tanyard, containing 64 pits and vats, many of them nearly new, and connected together on the most improved plan; with a Green Hide House, large and new built Leather House, Work House, and complete Drying Chambers over the whole two open drying sheds . . . The purpose of a Tanner has been carried on here near a century, and for which purpose the property is admirably situated and adapted as an excellent and never failing stream of water adjoins the Tanyard."

On the Chapmangate side of the stream the Tanyard consisted of 27 pits and vats, a large BARK HOUSE and BARK MILL. Pits and vats were used by the tanners to dip the animal hides in different strengths of solution of the tanning agent - tannic acid. Tannic acid was obtained from the crushed and powdered bark of oak trees when water was added. Hence the requirement for the Bark House and the Bark Mill. These two buildings were without doubt the main buildings of the mill, now demolished.

Between 1833 and 1845 the tanyards were purchased by Robert Denison who gradually expanded the business until its failure in 1845.

By 1852 Robert Denison had turned the Tanyards in a FLAX business. The Bark House and Mill were re-equipped and extended for this venture. The main extension was to the left hand building, the main reason being that it now straddled the stream so that water power could be used. Evidence of the water wheel drive shafts could be seen - bricked up archways either side of the stream. Denison used Irish 'flaxdressers' in the mill.

In 1856 a large fire destroyed the mill's raw material, the flax stacks, situated near the railway station down Cemetery Lane. The buildings never fully recovered from the loss and also mismanagement, so that by 1860 the Flax Mill had ceased trading.

About 1860 the Flax Mill was bought by Thomas Grant, who was to become the major builder of Victorian Pocklington. He used the mill as a warehouse for his building materials, glass and porcelain.

One night in March 1896 fire broke out in the Chapmangate area of Pocklington. The roof of the main body of the mill (left hand building) was destroyed. The walls of the building were left intact apart from the gables. An extensive report on the fire appeared in the Pocklington Weekly News of 21st March 1896.

Pocklington had no fire service of its own so buckets were used until the York Horse-drawn steam-powered fire tender arrived. Also the N.E.R. Fire train was used. The estimated loss to Thomas Grant and R. M. English was put at between £5,000 and £10,000. R. M. English had his mill where today's Post Office stands. This mill was undamaged but his warehouses were lost. The cost of extinguishing the fire was put at £60 or £70. Some men were paid 1s 8d per hour and a local councillor stated that it was 'a howling shame' that such high rates had been set!

Within days of the fire, in <u>April 1896,</u> Thomas Grant had been elected to the Town Council. He was a man of great vision for he proposed turning his burnt-out warehouse into an up-to-date PUBLIC HALL. So it transpired that the warehouse became the 'Victoria Hall' in 1896, although it was not opened until May 1987 in honour of Queen Victoria's Diamond Jubilee. R. M. English, also a local councillor, proposed buying the hall. The cost was put at between £800 and £900. He envisaged using it as either a Police Station or a Public Swimming Pool. The swimming pool idea was vetoed due to the estimated cost of £1000. In the end Grant refused to sell and he operated it until the mid 1920's as a public hall. Operas, Balls, Concerts, Plays and Regimental Dinners were all held in the Hall. Its final public uses were as a Dance Hall and Cinema. It then became the mill owned by R. M. English and was demolished late 1989.

The Office.

This was built by Thomas Grant and opened in May 1897 by R. M. English. It was built as an up-to-date and model office/warehouse. It is basically unaltered to this day.

The Pet Shop.

This was built in the mid 1700's as a workers home for those employed at the Tanyard. The building has been extended but the original house is largely intact.

TERRIFIC FIRE AT POCKLINGTON
STIRRING SCENES – UNTOLD DAMAGE
BY AN EYE WITNESS
WEEKLY NEWS OFFICE, EARLY HOURS, SATURDAY MORNING

The dreaded catastrophe has happened. A fearful fire has burst out at Pocklington, and for a time half the town seemed at the mercy of the pitiless flames. At the time of writing, the conflagration has been got under control and the awful possibilities of four o'clock have fortunately been dispersed. The scene of the fire was the extensive buildings in Chapmangate, which constitute the Salvation Army Barracks, and comprise also the extensive corn warehouses of Mr. R. M. English, Auctioneer and Corn Merchant, and the building warehouses of Mr. Thomas Grant.

Mr. William Tinson, builder, who lives opposite the scene of the conflagration was the first to discover the outbreak at half past three and with commendable promptitude he roused the sleeping town, and then went to knock up Mr. English. Meanwhile Mr. Thomas Robson, Solicitor, who lives in the same vicinity, was soon up, and first thought of having the Church bells rung to give a general alarm. As numbers of people now appeared at the scene, this proceeding was rendered superfluous. He did the next best thing, therefore, and despatched Mr. Lister as mounted messenger for the Fire Brigade at York.

The readier means of communication had also been availed of, both at the Railway Station, by Mr. F. Todd, and at the Post Office, by Mr. T. Scaife, and the Fire Brigade at York was conjured to arrive with all possible speed. Word had also been sent to the Fire Brigades at Beverley and Market Weighton. By this time the fire, which had burst out at the staircase doorway and entrance, was growing in intensity and extent, fanned by a gentle wind from the south west, and soon the building was one mass of flames.

It was soon evident that the premises were irretrievably doomed, and the anxiety now was to prevent the flames from igniting the contiguous property. The heat in Chapmangate was unbearable, and may be readily imagined when we state that the windows in Boyes Terrace, directly opposite, were cracked and broken in all directions, whilst the woodwork was charred and smoking. Willing helpers were to hand, and with great zeal dashed hundreds of buckets of water on the frontages to allay the heat.

Time wore on, and the wind veered round to another quarter, and threatened the very extensive warehouses belonging to Mr. Thomas Grant, builder. An antiquated manual pump was at once requisitioned and a connection established with the beck, and a small hose was brought to play its little part in trying to arrest the spreading of the devouring element.

Meanwhile Chapmangate presented a busy scene, a large number of volunteers working like Trojans under the superintendance of Mr. English, who, amidst the scene of devastation preserved admiral self control and gave his instructions in a manner which energized all within hearing. Hundreds of pounds worth of corn seeds and other grains were stored in the warehouses, and by dint of tremendous exertion, scores of bags were rescued from destruction.

As the flames showed no abatement, the inhabitants of the adjoining cottages realised the peril of their position, and by Herculean efforts, the household furniture and effects were speedily transferred to cooler quarters in the main street. The conglomeratin of articles piled at hazard in the centre of the road was a thing to wonder at.

Still no fire engine! At the rear of the conflagration a similar scene was being enacted, Mr. Grant and a gang of workers removing, with the utmost rapidity, the combustible articles reposited in the warehouse. Matters looked increasingly serious as the flames shot their lurid tongues in all directions, and still no fire engine had arrived. At length, at five minutes to six, the City fire manual engine appeared in Chapmangate, and amid much cheering, made its way to the back of the conflagration, where it was raging most furiously. Fortunately, a capital supply of water was at hand, with two jets at work, under the leadership of Inspector Morrell and Sergeant Alp, and soon made an impression. Nearly a mile of hose was available so that one jet could be directed to the front of the premises and the other to the rear. Amid crackling timbers, shattered crockery, burning embers, and tottering walls, the men played on the fiery mass with ever more effect and soon the danger of the flames spreading further was entirely dissipated. At about seven o'clock, the North Eastern Railway Brigade from York, under the superintendance of Assistant Superintendant Carline, and Captain Dow, arrived by special train, with 2,500 yards of hose and a No. 1 steamer and made assurance doubly sure. They got word of the fire at five minutes to five, but in consequence of the line being blocked and a pilot engine having to precede them it was not until quarter past six that they got away. Arrived at Pocklington with steam up, they soon had four jets playing on the now smouldering ruins, and completely subdued the smoking embers at least for a time.

The loss sustained must be enormous, and has variously been estimated at from £5,000 to £10,000. We understand that Mr. English's property was to a large extent covered by insurance. It is said that Mr. Grant's property was fully insured. In the latter premises were stored a large quantity of costly carved oak, valuable old and new crockery, and books, and the loss to the owner must be incalculable.

The wrecked premises, also comprised a lodge room rented by the Good Templars, and, in addition to their expensive regalia, they have lost a lot of valuable crockery.

The origin of the conflagration is a mystery. All that is known is that the Salvation Army held a service on the premises last night, and a fire was in the grate, but as to whether the outbreak can be traced to that cause is yet to be ascertained. All was left safe at nine o'clock last night.

THANKS

Mr. English authorises us to express his thanks to the large band of workers, who, at no little personal risk, worked wonders at saving goods and arresting the spread of the flames. We are sure that these sentiments will be endorsed by Mr. Grant, and we should like to bear our testimony to the splendid heroism and arduous labour which was manifested by a large number of townspeople and others.

A couple of Pocklington cyclists did good service by going to York on their tandem to ascertain the movements of the Fire Brigade. They accomplished their journey in capital time, in spite of a spill, and a welcome feeling of relief was experienced whey they reported the City Brigade was on its way, thus quietening the fear that half the town would be involved.

The City Brigade was driven by four horses, and the fire gallop was maintained all the way to the scene of action. The initial delay was caused by endeavours to secure a special train, which, however, they could not get in time to effect any appreciable advantage.

Thoughtfully enough, Councillor Cundall remembered the inner wants of the now tired and hungry firemen, and caused a breakfast to be provided for them at the Feathers Hotel.

March, 1896

THE GREAT FIRE AT POCKLINGTON

As previously reported in our special fire edition, Pocklington, last Saturday morning, came perilously near to being consumed "HOLUS BOLUS". The fire broke out in Messrs. Grant and English's warehouse, in Chapmangate, about half past three in the morning, and before the fire brigade from York arrived the premises were reduced to ruins and the flames spread with appalling vigour to the adjoining property. However, Herculean local effort, combined with the assistance of a powerful engine and manual from York, succeeded in arresting flames, and once more the urgent need at once to procuring adequate fire coping appliances was evident. The damage is estimated at between £5,000 and £10,000. Mr. Grant, who was insured in the Imperial Fire Office, has already come to an arrangement with the office in respect of the damage he sustained, and other persons who suffered from the ravages of the flames have also had their claims satisfied.

March, 1896

EMBERS

Relics of the conflagration, in the shape of melted glass, etc., were eagerly sought after. Last big blaze at Pocklington was 40 years ago, when huge flax stacks were consumed, the blaze being sufficient to light up houses at Market Weighton, 7 miles distant.

March, 1896

Lyndhurst – The home of R. M. English built by Thomas Grant

"A HINT"
– Letter to the Pocklington Weekly News

Dear Sir,

I have heard it rumoured that Councillor Grant proposed turning his burnt out warehouse into an up to date "Public Hall". When we note how badly off we are for such a building we cannot help but admire the public spirit of this resolve and, as the fire seemed to cure the town, it may turn out to be a blessing in disguise. I would suggest there be one or two ante-rooms attached, in which any small meetings might conveniently be held.

Thanking you in anticipation,
Old Pocklingtonian

April, 1896

RENEWED OUTBREAK OF FIRE AT POCKLINGTON

Last Saturday afternoon, a portion of the embers in Mr. Grant's warehouse, which had been smouldering ever since the fire, broke out again. Assistance was soon at hand and a few buckets of water completely extinguished the fire. Watchers, however, sat up all night.

April, 1896

CURIOUS

The Market Weighton Fire Brigade do not admit that they were summoned to the Pocklington blaze, and yet they received a telegram countermanding the alleged summons to come to Pocklington. We have received a long private letter on the subject, in which the writer deprecates the action of some anonymous correspondent who wanted to know why the summons had not been responded to. Until a summons has been proved, it was certainly unjust to condemn the Market Weighton Fire Brigade, who we are sure, would have done all in their power to render assistance to their neighbours in distress.

April, 1896

PHOTOGRAPHS
Mr. Tayleure, photographer, of Pocklington, improved the "shining hour" by taking capital photographs of the ruins of the burnt out warehouses. They are now on sale and will prove interesting souvenirs in times to come.

April, 1896

A NEW PUBLIC HALL AT POCKLINGTON
As we intimated a few months ago, the reconstruction of Mr. Thomas Grant's burnt out warehouse into an up to date and commodious public hall is progressing rapidly and we are now able to announce that the opening of the new hall is expected to take place on May 12th when the Choral and Orchestral Society will give their Spring concert, for which the finest vocalists from the North of England have been engaged.

5th March, 1897

OPENING OF THE VICTORIA HALL
From a charred and dismantled warehouse, Councillor Thomas Grant's premises in Chapmangate have been transmogrified into a handsome, spacious, and comfortable public hall. Inside, appearance and accoustic properties, as well as in the important matters of exits and ante-rooms, the new building is all that could be desired, and so far as the interior of the structure goes it would be a credit to a far more pretentious town than Pocklington. The exterior might be considerably improved but if, we have the picture, the frame is only of secondary importance, and we have no doubt in the future years the desired transformation will be affected in this respect also. The Hall will be opened on Thursday when the Choral and Orchestral Society will give the 4th concert, which will consist of a performance of Handel's "ACIS and GALITEA" and a miscellaneous second half. First class soloists are announced for the principle parts, and we doubt not that the event will in every way be on a scale quite befitting so auspicious an occasion. An excursion on that date will be run from Hull and Beverley, and Market Weighton, returning from Pocklington at 11.22 pm.

8th May, 1897

FORMATION OF THE POCKLINGTON FIRE BRIGADE
FIRE BRIGADE FOR POCKLINGTON?
Almost to a day last year, we had an urgent leader on the necessity for at once providing fire appliances. There is now some talk of at once providing a fire brigade, volunteers would not be wanting, all the sufferers from the fire have had a great deal of sympathy expressed to them. More than 1,000 of the Fire Editions of this paper, the Weekly News, were sold; the advertisers got their moneys worth.

March, 1896

AFTER THE FIRE

POCKLINGTON URBAN COUNCIL – The Surveyor reported that a representative of Messrs. Merryweather, fire engine makers, had called upon him, and the outcome of the interview was that the firm had offered to lend for £2 inclusive, proper appliances with which to test, in various parts of the town, the efficiency of the water supply for the purpose of extinguishing fires. If a purchase ensued no charge for the loan would be made. It was resolved to take advantage of the firm's offer. An offer from Messrs. Harrison and Co., Pocklington to supply a steam engine and appliances was allowed to stand over.

April, 1896

FIRE APPLIANCE

The Surveyor reported to Pocklington Council that there were only seven hydrants in the streets, and that to reach the buildings in the town, as a whole, they would require, in some cases, nine chains of hose and two standpipes and he, therefore, offered Messrs. Merryweather of London £2 for the loan of necessaries and 600 feet of hose. The firm had replied that £2 was quite inadequate, but to meet the Council, they would lend the appliances free, on their paying carriage, and returning the hose in good condition. They would also make special copper branch pipes to fit the hydrants. In reply to his enquiries the Water Company had promised to do anything to assist them in their proposed fire tests, provided that there was no undue waste of water. He would be glad if the Council would arrange a date for the tests. If the Council required Engine or Appliances, they would no doubt invite firms to send in prices.

May, 1896

AFTER THE FIRE THE FLOOD

What with WIND and what with WATER, Pocklington Market Place yesterday afternoon was a sight to be remembered. It was the occasion of the testing of the water hydrants in the town, preparatory to taking further steps in the matter of providing necessary means of coping with an outbreak of fire. For the experiment, special hose and standpipes had been lent by Messrs. Merryweather and Co. and the arrangements were capitally carried out by Mr. G. H. Gibson, Surveyor. Mr. Green was road foreman and Mr. William Tinson rendered most valuable assistance. The water from the reservoir was only drawn upon, and otherwise, conditions were quite normal. The first object of attack was the York Union Bank, on which were directed two hoses connected with hydrants in the Market Place and New Street, respectively, both drawn from the same mains. After a slight contratemps, due to the bursting of hose, capital supplies were secured playing on the building from both hoses, the water reached to top most roof. Operations were then transferred to the National Schools, New Street, George Street, and Chapmangate, where sufficient pressure was secured to reach the highest premises with ease. George Street perhaps offered the least pressure, owing to the main being only a 3 inch, as compared with the 5 inch main in the Market Place. Despite vigorous atempts, the firemen "were not able to reach the Church clock" which might have suffered a severe shock from such an unwanted shower bath. The experiments ceased at the White Mills, and the afternoon trial must have given the Council plenty of AQUEOUS evidence to work upon.

May, 1896

THE WATER TESTS – OFFICIAL REPORT

The Surveyor, Mr. G. H. Gibson, reported on the hydrant tests as follows. I had the Water Company's supply of water tested with the appliances supplied to us by Messrs. Merryweather of London. Prior to attaching the hose, I tested the pressure at the different hydrants in the town with a patent water gauge and found it to vary from 40 lbs to the square inch at the hydrant opposite the Elms, to 35 lbs opposite Mr. Todd's house in George Street. He had found to cut off the supply from Givendale barely diminished the pressure by a pound, and therefore determined to make the test with the water from Givendale cut off, depending on the reservoir supply only. Although we have had so much dry weather, the reservoir was running over to begin with, and he calculated that during the whole experiment they were running an amount of water off equal to one jet from a half inch nozzle for a continuous period of one and a half hours, and that we used 60 gallons per minute. At the end of the experiment I visited the reservoir, and found that we had used 8 inches in depth of water, and that there was still 10 ft 2 in of water in stock, so that we might have kept the hose in operation over 15 hours before running the water off the reservoir alone, independant of the Givendale supply.

I would suggest that the Highways Committee be instructed to gain prices and specifications for fire engines and appliances, and to report at the next meeting.

May, 1896

AFTER THE FIRE

The Highways Committee recommended that certain fire coping appliances be purchased for a good round sum, which, it was suggested should not be divulged for the present. It was suggested that certain hose, standpipes, etc., should be bought as they would be required in any case.

Councillor Thomas said the bill for extinguishing the late fire amounted to between £60 and £70, some of the men being paid at the rate of 1s.8d. per hour. He thought it was a burning shame that such an exorbitant rate should be paid. The Chairman said the Pumpers got but 1s. per hour "we were glad to have them at any price". Councillor Thomas said there were several bottles of whisky and gin charged for, he did not know who had ordered them and, of course, it was immaterial to the Council.

June, 1896

HYDRANT EQUIPMENT

Detailed statement for a "hydrant" equipment was laid before the Council. Amongst the appliances mentioend were 700 feet of hand made hose, swivel couplings, double outlets, swivel standpipes, three hose clamps, branch pipe supports, five portable fire ladders, and two branch pipes. In reply to Councillor English, the Surveyor said that in the event of the "engine" being obtained in the future, the hose now being recommended could easily be adapted.

With regard to the fire engine, it was stated again that a fire might break out at Millington, Warter or elsewhere, and they might charge for the service just as Pocklington had had to pay for the York Brigade. If an engine was gone in for they were strongly in favour of a "Steam Engine" as it was much more efficient and was independent of manual assistance. The Committee were quite prepared to submit estimates and particulars for a complete fire engine and equipment if it was desired. The Chairman said that the feeling was for an engine of some kind.

June, 1896

A STEAM FIRE ENGINE FOR POCKLINGTON

At the last meeting of the Pocklington Urban District Council this urgent and important subject came up for discussion and consideration and the following report was read.

Fire Appliances – this matter having been referred back to the Highway Committee for further consideration, the latter, having made enquiries, found that one of the latest pattern of Messrs. Merryweather Manual Engines had been found to have been supplied to the Urban District Council at Gainsborough, Lincolnshire and after arrangements had been made with the officials, it was decided to proceed there and see the engine at work. On Monday 26th October, therefore, a deputation consisting of the following members of the Highways Committee, Messrs. Smith, Brigham, Thirsk, and the Clerk and the Surveyor, went to Gainsborough. The Chairman of the Water Works Committee and the Surveyor of Gainsborough had arranged for a rare public display in the Market Place, but before this took place, the Committee was shown over the main Fire Station where they found one of Messrs. Merryweather's Steam Fire Engines, which had been procured some 15 years earlier, and which was now in practically as good condition as when purchased. The manual engine at Gainsborough was one that had been arranged to be worked by 22 men, and had a capacity of delivering ordinarily 100 gallons per minute, but being provided with plenty of handle room and being stronger manned a similar engine had discharged 142 gallons per minute. The manual engine had been purchased as an auxilliary to the "steamer", it having happened at Gainsborough two fires at the same time, and the manual is kept more in the centre of the town for immediate action. Most of the fireman are employees of Messrs. Marshall and Son, and only 15 were able to turn out to man the engine on this occasion. They were men of fine physique and worked very hard, but it was evident that being a third of their complement short, the work was far too exhausting for them and it was certain that with only 15 men there would have to be a fresh set every 10 minutes. The men soon formed themselves into position, and in 33 seconds from the signal given, they were playing on the highest building in the Market Place. Through a three quarter inch nozzle I estimate that the work would be effective at a height of 50 feet. Through a half inch hozzle it was possible to send the water 120 feet high, but at that height it seemed little more than spray, and would have had little effect on a fire. The water supply was from the street hydrant and into a portable canvass dam, similar to the one quoted us. After the display in the Market Place, the men showed us the use of the Patent Respirator which enables a person to breathe through the densest smoke. The Captain informed us that he had been a quarter of an hour in a building with one of the respirators where brimstone and chalk straw were burning, and had felt no worse for his experience. For our benefit a fire of damp straw and rubbish was made in the stable belonging to the Council, and the place was soon full of the blackest smoke. Into this building went 2 firemen and the Medical Officer of Health and they were able to remain in for 4 minutes, without injury. It is quite certain that without the respirator no person would have kept in for 30 seconds without being suffocated. The Highways Committee are favourable to obtaining 3 of these respirators.

After the display in the Market Place, we met the officials at a hotel and had a long discussion with them as to the relative advantages of the manual and steam fire engines, and they all concurred in recommending the purchase of a steam fire engine on the following grounds:-

1) Effectiveness - from a steam engine there is a constant and invariable pressure, at least 3 times the maximum from a manual engine. It was pointed out that it is the force at which the water goes that extinguishes the fire more than the quantity discharged. It was also pointed out that in country districts, where water is frequently considerable distances from the fire, the strength of the men is exhausted in getting the water through the hose, while the force of the water at the nozzle end is thus diminished to almost nothing.

2) Expense and the difficulty of securing men to work a manual engine. At least 44 men would be required to work in shifts say of 10 minutes. This would mean for a 3 hour fire 6 guineas, whereas 2 men will work the steam engine and the cost of fuel, oil, etc., would not be more than 2s 6d per hour.

Careful enquiries as to the cost of the maintenance of the fire engine at Gainsborough were made, and it was found that the expense of the upkeep of both manual and steam engine did not exceed 3s 6d per week, while as I have already pointed out the steam engine there has not perceptibly deteriorated in a space of 15 years.

The Committee feel very much indebted to the Gainsborough Officials for their kindness and trouble in giving every information and having given the matter the fullest consideration, have come to the conclusion unanimously to recommend to the Council the purchase of the steam engine offered by Messrs. Merryweather and Sons, of London, which is an engine of the newest design, all the latest improvements, and capable ordinarily of discharging 200 gallons per minute to a height of 100 feet through $1/_2$ mile of hose. Every necessary requisite and appliance is supplied with the engine, and in addition to this all the appliances for use with the street hydrants are included, and these latter, Council are advised to purchase at once so that the town can be protected to, at least, this extent against fire. The Committee have also considered the matter of housing the engine and unanimously recommend the brick shed, with a slate roof in the stone yard at the end of the existing shed adjoining the footpath. Plans and specifications have been prepared for this shed, and the Committee have instructed me to apply to the 3 builders in the town for a price, and if agreeable to the Council, I will accept the lowest tender when I receive them. As to payment of the engine, an estimate has been made, and it is found that the whole affair is paid for by 15 annual instalments of principle and interest combined, for 3% interest, and allowing for 3/- per week maintenance, an annual 1p rate in the £ on the whole on the rateable value will clear the thing. But Gainsborough have a better way of maintaining their engines than by charging it wholly on the rates, and it is submitted by your Committee that this could well be attempted by the Council. To all villages in the neighbourhood requiring the services of the Brigade, according to the size and rateable value, a fee of from 1 guinea to 3 guineas per annum is charged, and for this amount any subscribing village can, in the case of fire, use the fire engine for just out of pocket expenses.

Councillor Smith endorsed the report. Councillor Thirsk said he was now in favour of a steam fire engine instead of a manual. The steam engine would eventually cost them less than a manual. Another point was that they could not borrow money for a manual, but they could for a steam engine, the payment of which might be spread over 15 years. On the motion of Councillor English, seconded by Councillor Thomas, it was unanimously decided to obtain a steam fire engine and it was ultimately decided to purchase the steam fire engine, together with appliances mentioned in the foregoing report. It was further decided that the expenses incurred by the deputation to Gainsborough, £4 17s 2d, to be paid by the Council. Further it was decided to make an application to the Local Government Board to borrow £500 for 20 years to purchase the fire extinguishing appliances.

November, 1896

FIRE ENGINE SHED

Last night, December 4th, 1896, Pocklington Urban District Council accepted the tender of Mr. W. Tinson for the erection of a shed for the fire engine, cost £49.

– One Week later – In response for applications for the erection of a Fire Engine Shed, only one builder, Mr. William Tinson, submitted a tender for the above. As reported last week, it was agreed to accept the amount, being £49 15s 0d. Councillor Smith said the amount was a larger one than they had expected and not one of them would vote readily for it but they appeared to have no alternative.

December 4th, 1896

EDITOR'S COMMENT

Supplementing our report, the editor of the Pocklington Weekly News wishes it to be known the tender by Mr. William Tinson of £49 15s for the proposed fire engine shed is considered very reasonable for the work required. Surprise is expressed that he would do it for that amount.

December, 1896

FIRE ENGINE DELIVERY?

Mr. Gibson, Urban Surveyor, has received a letter from Messrs. Merryweather and Sons of London, stating that the new steam fire engine, which that firm has built for the Pocklington Urban Council, has now gone into the paint shop, and will be ready for delivery next week. The weather, however, has been so unfavourable for building operations that it has prevented the contractor, Mr. W. Tinson, from getting further than the foundations for the new engine shed, and until that is complete, the engine will not be got down to Pocklington.

January, 1897

ANOTHER OUTBREAK OF FIRE AT POCKLINGTON
– a house reeking with smoke

On Wednesday noon an outbreak of fire occurred at premises on New Pavement, Pocklington, and had it not been for the timeous discovery the whole block might have been gutted by the merciless flames. A portion of premises is referred to as occupied by Mr. Charles Hotham, butcher, whilst the remainder is tenanted by a widow named Mrs. Hunter, and it was in the latter's house where the outbreak occurred. Mrs. Hotham first smelt of burning, and being strongly impressed that something was amiss, she prevailed upon her husband to investigate the matter, Mrs. Hunter being out of her house at the time. Mr.Hotham gained access to the house, and traced the fire to a cupboard in the kitchen. Apparently, a brick had fallen out of the chimney, causing the stoothing to be ignited, and the stoothing in turn had set fire to a large canister of corks, which smelt villainousley, not to mention the fact that a blaze of fire had already burst out. Mr. Hotham quickly obtained a little assistance, and half a dozen well directed pails full of water soon subdued the rising flames.

January, 1897

THE WATER WORKS AND FIRE HYDRANTS

The Surveyor had been in correspondence with the Clerk to the Water Company as to the supply of additional fire hydrants, and the Company quoted £4 10s each for them fixed complete, and an annual rent charge of 10/- each, or they were willing to put them in without any additional cost to the Council at annual rent of £1 per annum each. It seemed to him that the former quote was the best option for the Council.

March, 1897

POCKLINGTON FIRE APPLIANCE
LOCAL GOVERNMENT BOARD INQUIRY –

The Urban Council of Pocklington have applied to the Local Government Board for sanction to borrow £500 for fire extinguishing apparatus. The local Government Board met, yesterday, under the presidency of Lt. Col. A. C. Smith, at the Council Chamber, Railway St., Pocklington. The usual formalities having been complied with, specifications of the machine were submitted. These showed that it was of Mr. Merryweather's Patent Light County Council Steam Fire Engines, capable of delivering 200 gallons of water and consisting of a patent vertical boiler as adopted by the Metropolitan Fire Brigade etc., the tubes are solid drain made of copper giving perfect circulation. The steam can be raised from cold water in 3 minutes and to working pressure in 6 or 8 minutes from time of lighting fire. It is provided with safety valves and all necessary fittings of high finish. The carriage frame is of wrought iron mounted on high spoke wood wheels. The engine and boiler are secured to the frame by such a manner as to relieve them from any strain whilst travelling. The frame also carried a capacious box for hose and implements and affords accommodation for several men. The engine is complete in its self and the machinery is placed vertically in front of the boile . The pump is of gun metal and a continuous flow is obtained, enabling the engine to throw a compact and steady jet. The necessary fittings are provided together with a double lever brake for hind wheels, 4 x 8ft lengths of vulcanised suction hose, 5 x 100ft lengths of delivery hose, 3 leather hose clamps for stopping leakages while at work, 1 brass helmet and 6 leather helmets, 7 pairs of leggings, total cost £363.

The next question was the engine shed which will be constructed by taking down a workshop and building a new shed for the fire engine in the stoneyard near the West Green railway crossing at Pocklington. The technical specifications were submitted and eventually the Inspector was taken on a tour of the town that he might fully understand the needs and requirements for the place. Plans for the position of the engine shed and water mains etc., were also submitted. The Inspector left Pocklington by the 11 am train to York.

April, 1897

FIRE BRIGADE CHARGES

The Lighting and Fire Brigade Committee, recommend that the organisation of the Fire Brigade to be performed in connection with the "new engine" be under the control of the Council. That the scale of charges be:-

1st hour each officer 5/- and each hour afterwards 2s 6d, each fireman 1st hour 3/- and afterwards 2/- per hour. That the following persons to be asked to form a Brigade with power to add to their numbers – Captain, Mr. T. W. Calverley-Rudston (JP), Superintendent Mr. J. H. Gibson (Surveyor), Engineer Mr. Summerson (Clerk to the Council), Deputy Engineer Mr. Joe Green (Road Foreman), Hose Superintendent Mr. WIlliam Tinson (Builder), Firemen – Mr. John Robson, Mr. Thomas English, A. Rapp, R. I. Young, J. Fielder, Thomas Haggard, Councillor Proctor, Charles Buttle.

May 1897

LOAN

The loan of £500 at 3% for the payment of the fire equipment offered by Mr. R. M. English was accepted by the Pocklington Urban Council.

June, 1897

FIRE AT FOGGATHORPE

Stackyards in flames – Pocklington Brigade to the rescue.

On Thursday morning at 8.30 Mr. G. H. Gibson, Superintendent of the Pocklington Fire Brigade, received a telegram from Mr. Chaplin of the Black Swan Hotel, Foggathorpe, which read, quote "Gibson, Haystack fire at Black Swan, Foggathorpe, come at once. CHAPLIN". Mr. Gibson is agent for the Alliance Insurance Company with whom Mr. Chaplin's house, buildings and agricultural projects are insured and it became an open question as to whether Mr. Chaplin required the services of the fire brigade or Mr. Gibson as insurance agent.

Mr. Gibson decided it was not advisable to send the brigade, however, it was decided that cyclists be sent to the scene of the fire to see whether the fire was extinguished and whether there was any water available, with instructions to telegraph from BUBWITH. Once receiving the telegram the brigade was summoned with all haste and very speedily the engine and brigade were on their way to Foggathorpe via SEATON ROSS. The entire distance being covered in 50 minutes.

On arrival they were saluted with the information that the fire had been extinguished by the SELBY brigade, the journey made fruitless. Not so, however, the long arm of coincidence now came into view. The numbers in the brigade were

POCKLINGTON

URBAN DISTRICT COUNCIL

FIRE BRIGADE

Scale of Charges to be made for the use of the Steam Fire Engine, Brigade, and Appliances.

	£	s.	d.
To Engine turning out	1	1	0
„ Use of Engine from arrival at the Fire to return to Fire Station, per hour	0	10	0
„ Use of Hose Pipes, &c., ditto ditto, per hour	0	5	0
„ Messenger summoning Brigade . . .	0	5	0
„ Cleaning Engine and Hose Pipes . . .	0	10	0

„ Captain, Superintendent, and Engineer, each 5/- for first hour, and 2/6 every subsequent hour, from time of summons to return to Fire Station.

„ Firemen, each 3/- for first hour, and 2/- every subsequent hour.

„ Hire of Horses—amount actually paid.

The above scale applies only to Fires in Parishes which subscribe annually to the maintenance of the Fire Brigade, as follows:—viz., Parishes of a less rateable value than £2000, One Guinea; all other Parishes, Two Guineas.

Double the above charges will be made for attending Fires in non-subscribing Parishes; and the Captain and Superintendent are empowered to refuse to allow the attendance of the Brigade at any such Fires.

It is of essential importance that persons summoning the Brigade should state the distance from the Fire of the nearest water supply, and the nature of such supply.

All applications must be made to the Superintendent, Mr. GEORGE H. GIBSON, Regent Street, Pocklington. Telegraphic Address, "Gibson, Pocklington."

By order of the Council,

ALFRED SUMMERSON,
CLERK.

Pocklington, 16th October, 1897.

The first Fire Engine - Pocklington 1897

just having some refreshment when up rode a mounted messenger with news of another blaze at Mr. Townsley's farm. Up went the brigade, there at the farm was a huge stack of hay, the produce of over 37 acres, burning like matchwood. This was serious enough, but worst feature of it was the farm buildings were only some two yards away. A gentle breeze was not assisting matters. However, connections were made with the nearest pond and water was soon flowing through the hose. However, in two hours or more the pond was exhausted and Mr. Townsley telegraphed for the Selby fire brigade to come again, in order to reach a further pond with their additional hose.

They arrived before 2 pm and by pumping water into a rain tub, from the further pond, they enabled the Pocklington Brigade to keep on a continuous pressure. Soon the second pond was exhausted and a wire was sent for more hose to reach a third pond at the brickyards. The hose arrived by train, and the water was pumped from the brickyard pond into the farmyard pond for a night supply in case of further outbreaks. The Selby Brigade left at midnight, after a consultation, the Pocklington Brigade was left in charge. The fire had been practically mastered for sometime, but it broke out thrice again, and eventually about 50 cartloads of smouldering hay had to be led away to make safety a certainty. The Pocklington Brigade arrived home at 8.30 am. The engine did its work in a very efficient manner. Nearly everyone was drenched to the skin, some were so bedraggled and begrimed as to almost lose their identities. Mr. Townsley and household were most attentive to wants and comforts of the Brigade. The estimate value of the consumed stack was £90.

August, 1897

Chapter VII

SPORTING NEWS

ICE HOCKEY – KILNWICK

Grammar School v Town. This match came off at the Kilnwick Fish Pond under conditions which could not be termed other than ideal. The ice was in good condition, and there was area in plenty for the players to follow the game without let or hindrance either to themselves or others. The weather was superb, and the grand stretch of ice was covered with a moving throng of the wearers of the steels. Final score Town 9 goals, School 7 goals.

February, 1895

CYCLING PRIZE – POCKLINGTON

Through the medium of "REFEREE" (a paper) a handsome gold medal will be offered to any cyclist residing in Pocklington, or within a radius of 8 miles, who by the 31st August, shall hold the record officially timed between the West Green railway gates, Pocklington, and the railway bridge, Market Weighton.

May, 1895

POCKLINGTON ATHLETES TO THE FORE

At the Beverley sports on Wednesday, Mr. R. Young, of Pocklington, succeeded in bringing off the first prize in the half mile flat handicap. Mr. J. Johnson, also of Pocklington, on the same evening, won the 100 yards flat handicap, after two dead heats, and was awarded a handsome cabinet, valued at £5-15-0. The following night Mr. Young won the one mile flat handicap; time 4 minutes 24 seconds.

June, 1895

COUNTY CRICKET

Oh Yorkshire, Yorkshire! You have a lot to answer for as the County Cricket XI. What hopes you have raised and expectations created only to crush them to earth, and to doom your supporters to disappointment. After your triumph but a fortnight ago over SURREY, as true TYKES put you down for the championship, and then out of pure cursedness you allow such Counties as ESSEX, GLOUCESTERSHIRE, and SOMERSET, to wipe the ground with you. Was ever such irony? Ah well! I suppose "glorious uncertainties" of cricket will always go hand in hand with "unglorious surprises". Oh, Yorkshire, Yorkshire!

August 1895

THE WEIGHTON CYCLING RECORD
– a splendid performance

On Wednesday night, G. A. Reade, of Market Weighton, had a shot for the road record between Weighton and Pocklington. The weather was all in his favour, and his performance is one that will take some beating. Starting from the Railway Bridge at Weighton, he was paced to Hayton, and got away at a rare speed. At Hayton, William Tanfield, took up the pacing and brought his man at a climbing pace to within easy distance of home, when P. Gibson completed the pacing to the West

Green Gates, where Reade passed through a large muster of spectators. He appeared to be in grand form, and at the conclusion of his ride, was not in the least exhausted. The time occupied was 18 minutes.

August, 1895

YORKSHIRE CYCLING RECORD BROKEN BY A GOOLE MAN

A. J. Wilson, started at 7 o'clock in the evening and was paced to Doncaster and then on to York. Unpaced he then went over a course which included Northallerton and Market Weighton. Between Selby and Scaith he was again picked up by a pacemaker, who took him to Doncaster and then back to Goole, by way of Bawtry, Thorne, and Rawcliffe. In the 24 hours it was found that he had ridden 286 miles, thus beating the previous record by 5 miles. He received two gold medals as reward.

September, 1895

AN ASSOCIATION FOOTBALL CLUB FORMED AT POCKLINGTON

As the outcome of a widely expressed desire for a club which would use to the best advantage the association football talent of the town, such an organisation has been formed, founded on a sound basis, to be conducted on purely businesslike and gentlemanly principles. A meeting was held during the week at which it was decided to call the new venture the "Pocklington Wednesday Association Football Club", Dr. Angus Fairweather being elected as Captain. The colours are to be navy blue and white, whilst the field wil be dependent on what the Rugby Club decide upon.

September, 1895

CROWD VIOLENCE AT POCKLINGTON

RUGBY – The match last Saturday was played in too hot weather for good football. At times, however, the Pocklington backs showed splendid combination and passing powers and, if in future the forwards will only let the ball come out, they need have no fear but that the backs will score. it is a pity that the game was marred by an instance of rough play, but I think the spectators should keep off the field, and not incite the men in the manner they did last week.

September, 1895

POCKLINGTON TO THE FORE IN JOHANNESBURG

It is with great pleasure that we record the success of two Pocklington young men at Johannesburg. At the athletic sports held in connection with the Simmer and Jack Gold Mining Company, at Germiston, last Christmas Day, Mr. Sydney Steeles won the first prize in the sack race, and was awarded a splendid set of solid gold sleeve links and a set of solid gold studs. He also got third place in the hurdle race, and came in for a smokers combination as a prize. Mr. Reginald Steeles got second in the three legged race, and won a beautiful pair of tortoiseshell gold opera glasses.

January, 1896

PROPOSED CRICKET CLUB AT POCKLINGTON

On Monday night, a well attended meeting was held in the National Schools, kindly lent for the occasion, to consider the feasibility of forming a cricket club. There was a unanimous desire that a club should be formed, but the great difficulty was to secure a field. Several sites were suggested, eventually a deputation was appointed to Mr. Thirsk, with a view to obtaining the terms on which he would let HORSE AND FOAL SHOW field.

March, 1896

POCKLINGTON GOLF CLUB

The Pocklington Golf Club are to be congratulated on the site they have chosen for their links. Their park on the BALK lends itself readily to the formation of a thoroughly sporting course, abounding, as it does, in hazards of various kinds, such as ditches, trees, and hedges. The holes are 9 in number and vary ing length from 120 to 300 yards. With the exception of the greens, which are yet too rough for accurate putting, the course will be found quite equal to the majority of inland links. We understand that the secretary has received a goodly number of would be members.

October, 1896

POCKLINGTON LADY WINS IN SOUTH AFRICA

On Christmas Day, wars and rumours of wars from Johannesburg gave place to sports and social pleasure, and tears and fears to goodwill. Features for the days programme were races for ladies. In one of the open flat races for married ladies Mrs. Webb, nee Maggie Steeles, daughter of Mr. W. Steeles, won with ease out of nine competitors, and was awarded a handsome silver tea service, value 9 guineas. She was likewise an entrant in the egg and spoon race with five others, and came off victorious again, her reward being 4 silver salt cellars, valued at £5 15s.

January, 1897

HULL TO POCKLINGTON RUN

The Hull Racing Clubs postponed run to Pocklington came off on Saturday. The route was via Driffield, Wetwang, Fridaythorpe, and down the renowned Garrowby Hill.

Cyclists now experience considerable difficulty in traversing the hill, and the surface, having been washed into ridge by the water rushing down. As this continues for nearly three miles you can imagine the work that lay before the racing boys.

Those who participated in the outing were well repayed. On a clear day York Minster can be clearly seen, although 13 miles away. As you wind around the hill Bishop Wilton is visible and very pretty it looked on Saturday. The scenes across country were excellent. Having partaken of a good meal at the Feathers Hotel, Pocklington, and had a rest, the whole crew had a quite ride through Market Weighton and Beverley.

June, 1897

Chapter VIII

THE WEATHER

SEVERE WEATHER – POCKLINGTON

Owing to the severe weather of late, folk from Pocklington and other adjacent places had a rare struggle to reach the "Warter Ball" at the Priory. No fewer than 3 horses per carriage could negotiate Kilnwick Hill, and then it was a case of getting out and pushing or else leading the horses. Oh it was lively, if ever a cabbie earned his fee, it was on Tuesday night.

January, 1895

BECAUSE OF THE SNOW FALL – POCKLINGTON

Councillor Cundall said he had heard something about the labour in connection with clearing the snow not being judiciously used. Councillor Cundall had heard about 12 men working around one cart. Mr. Gibson, the surveyor, had said as a matter of fact 3 men were working around each cart and if the council would consult the wages book they would find this was the case. Councillor Powell said he had been told that a good many men had refused to work at removing the snow at the rate of 2/- per day; he would like to know if this were the case. The Surveyor replied that there had been such cases. The Surveyor stated that some of the outlying villages had cost between £40 -£50 to clear the snow whilst in Pocklington it had cost only 10 Guineas.

January, 1895

SNOWDRIFTS

The snow had drifted so terribly between HUNSLEY and NORTH CAVE that all traffic was impeded. 25 men were engaged in cutting the snow through DREWTON HILL at the foot of which it was drifted level with the hedges.

A Captain Philips was being conveyed from Beverley through to North Cave, but on reaching HUNSLEY he was compelled to discharge his conveyance and proceed to his destination on foot.

CRATHORNES flour waggon, which was drawn by four powerful horses, was landed in a snowdrift from which it could not be extricated. The men in attendance were compelled to unyoke and leave their charge until clearance was made.

January, 1895

CRICKET ON ICE – LUND

A cricket match, six a side, has been played on the ice at this village. The sides both wore skates, the game caused considerable amusement amongst the villagers.

February, 1895

CRICKET ON THE MERE – HORNSEA

On Saturday, a cricket match took place on the Mere, the sides being captained by Messrs. C. Cherry and W. Whiting respectively, which caused no small amount of interest.

A large crowd turned up to witness the play, which was very much enjoyed. It was regretted that such a late start was made, it being after 4 pm, owing to the snow which had fallen previously having to be swept away. During the match a SLEIGH with three gentleman, drawn by one horse, was parading about the ice.

February, 1895

Chapter IX

HEALTH

POCKLINGTON DISTRICT

Dr. Fairweather reported that the number of births registered during the year 1894 was 198, 99 were males and 99 females. During the same period there were 103 deaths, of these 40 were males and 63 females. The number of infectious diseases was 34, comprising 8 cases of TYPHOID, 22 fo SCARLETINA, 4 of ERISYPALIS.

February, 1895

DIPTHERIA AT HOWDEN

At the fortnightly meeting of the Rural District Council, Colonel Saltmarsh, Chairman, presided. It was reported by the Medical Officer of Health, that a serious outbreak of diptheria had occurred at Mr. Hairsines, Warwick House, Blacktoft, and in which four persons were suffering. The drinking water had been analysed, and was found to be very badly polluted, indeed so much so that it was totally unfit for domestic use. The sanitary conditions were also unsatisfactory. Certain precautions had been taken and disinfectants had been supplied.

January, 1895

TRIPLETS IN HULL

– The Queens bounty.

The vicar of Newington sends us the pleasing information that one of his parishioners, Mrs. Moody, 2 De la Pole Avenue, Hull, who on the 21st gave birth to triplets, all boys, has been the recipient of Her Majesty the Queens bounty of £3.

March, 1895

PILES

How many thousands of lives have been made miserable by the excrutiating complaint, it seems to break down the strongest man and spares none. The causes may be many, the cure is one Homocea. (HOMOCEA) instantly touches the spot and works marvels in a very short time.

February, 1895

Chapter X

COUNCIL WORK

NIGHT SOIL COLLECTION – HULL

Alderman Fraser, at a meeting of the Hull Corporation Sanitary Committee yesterday afternoon, raised the question of the adoption of the pail system for the collection of night soil. He said that under the system, the leakage from the carts would be ended because the pail would be removed, as it was. Dr. Mason and himself had made an inspection and they were assured by those who had already adopted the pails in their homes that they did not, under the new system, mind the night soil collector coming to their houses, because their removal did not lead to those offensive smells of which so much complaint had been made. The pails were not, in his opinion, an absolute cure. He thought the only satisfactory solution was the adoption of the water closet system.

February, 1895

POPULATION OF POCKLINGTON

Mr. Summerson, Clerk to the Council, stated that the population of Pocklington was 2,577 according to the census of 1891.

February, 1895

Open Beck (Sewer), Grape Lane, Pocklington

OBNOXIOUS SMELL IN POCKLINGTON

The recent rain seems to have had a deleterious effect upon the refuse passing through the town drains, and has resulted in the most obnoxious smells in various parts of the town.It is not the first time the matter has been reported, but from a sanitary point of view it is to be hoped the District Council will give the matter attention. Prevention is better than cure, and for the safety of the inhabitants it is hoped that the drains (which in most instances are recepticles for the various fever germs) will be examined without delay.

October, 1895

COUNCIL EMPLOYEES AND OUTSIDE WORK

Councillor Read said that he had heard that roadmen were sometimes allowed to go off for half a days threshing. If that was the case he thought it was hardly fair to those men who were out of work. Mr. Gibson, the surveyor, said that one of the men had asked to be off but he did not ask to be off to thresh. These men were only getting wages of 13/- a week at anytime. Ultimately the Surveyor was invested with discretionary powers in this matter.

February, 1895

ASPHALTING – POCKLINGTON

The Surveyor, Mr. Gibson, reported that pursuant to the instructions of the Highways Committee he had obtained two waggons of ASPHALT from the PATENT ASPHALT, LIMESTONE and CONCRETE COMPANY, BIRMINGHAM, and he had had the same layed down in the Market Place. At the suggestion of one of the Councillors he had prepared a statement of the costs and had found that the whole thing ran out to 1s 2d per square yard for material and labour. The Highways Committee had also directed the East side of Regent Street to be asphalted, and said had been done with material mixed at their own yard. With material and labour it ran at 101/2d per yard. Having carefully considered the matter he did not think the PATENT material was worth three pence halfpenny per square yard more than the home made asphalt and he would recommend that in future the latter be used.

August, 1896

SEWERAGE CONTRACTORS – POCKLINGTON

The Urban District Council of Pocklington invite tenders for the execution of the scheme for main sewerage disposal of the town of Pocklington. Contractors desirous of tendering must forward their names to the Engineer of Works, MR. BALFOUR.

August, 1896

SEWERAGE SCHEME - GOVERNMENT INQUIRY

On Tuesday, at the Court House, Pocklington, an inquiry was held into the application of the Urban District Council to construct a £5,000 Sewage Disposal Scheme.

The Clerk to the Council stated that the population of Pocklington at the 1891 census was 2,577 and the present rateable value was £5,486-16s-0d. He said that an amicable agreement had been reached by the Council with the Governors of Pocklington Grammar School for the purchase of land suitable for the sewerage

'Wilson the Grocer' circa 1895, Market Place, Pocklington. Now the 'Fruit Basket' Shop. Photograph taken by my great, great, great, great grandfather Michael Tayleure

works. The provisional agreement was lodged with the Charity Commissioners awaiting their sanction.

The new scheme was needed due to the defective state of the present system of drainage, the sewers discharging their contents into an open stream running through the town into a mill dam just outside the town and immediately in front of the Grammar School.

The Surveyor, Mr. Gibson, said that most of the drains of the existing system were of the "horse shoe pattern" and some had no bottom at all, others were field pipes and there were a few sanitary pipes. The contents of these drains ran into a stream running down the Market Place, through a brick culvert, which he believed had been built 70 years ago. Slop waters and the contents of about 30 water closets entered the drains. The connections were very bad, half of the horse shoe gulleys were full of decaying sewage. The worst feature of the whole system was that the sinks for taking away the surface water were in direct communication with the sewers and the foul gasses continually came up. He had frequent complaints of smells. The Clerk stated that the sum of £165 had been set aside for the cost of covering the stream.

Mr. Balfour, Engineer, then explained the scheme. He said it would consist of three and a half miles of glazed sanitary pipes, furnished with adequate means of ventilation and a large automatic flushing tank. The existing drains would be improved, and would be utilised to deal with the surface waters of the town. The sewage would first be treated in a chamber with ALUMINO-FERRIC, then pass through precipitating tanks in duplicate, having cross weir walls and coke filter cells. The clarified sewage would then be conveyed on to the land.

August, 1896

Junction of Percy Road - Kilnwick Road, Pocklington

GUIDE POSTS

In his report, the Surveyor to the Pocklington Rural District Council, said that in accordance with the Councils wishes, he had made an inspection of the roads in the District and found that it would require 23 NEW GUIDE POSTS, and 9 other posts would have to be repaired. The posts should be of good English oak, 10 feet long, 4 inches square, and 5 inches at the bottom, with arms 2ft 6in long, and 8in broad. The top of the posts to be pointed.

September, 1896

ALLEGED OVERCROWDING – POCKLINGTON

On the 18th September, the Surveyor, acting upon information he had received, visited a house in Waterloo Terrace and on visiting the place found a case of overcrowding. He was informed by the Occupier that he and his wife, plus another man and his wife, together with 5 children occupied the only bedroom in the house. The Surveyor served them with a Statutory 24 hour notice, requesting him to desist from having the bedroom crowded, and on visiting the house again he found that 1 of the beds had been removed into the living room, which was now overcrowded and in a dirty condition. He would suggest that the Council use its power to remedy this state of affairs. The Council decided that if the tenant did not comply with the Council's demands proceedings would be taken against him.

October, 1896

Hayton Bridge

HAYTON BRIDGE

The Chairman of the Council stated that the Bridge of Hayton was in a bad state of repair, and unless it was attended to, a collapse might occur at any time. This appeared to be the general feeling of the Council. Mr. Jacques said the bridge had been cracked for at least 20 years. Eventually it was decided to temporarily repair the bridge until it could be thoroughly overhauled.

October, 1896

ROADSIDE FIRES – A RISK

A list was submitted to the Pocklington Rural District Council by Inspector Rawlings who proposed to have notices affixed warning persons from camping and making fires in the highways and hedges. Not only did this practice constitute a danger to persons driving but great damage was wrought to hedges etc., by reason of their being pillaged for fuel. It was decided to have the notices put up forthwith.

October, 1896

MENAGERIE IN POCKLINGTON

On the 20th October, the proprietor of DAYS MENAGERIE asked for permission to stand his show in the Market Place, Pocklington. The entrance to the Green (the normal showground) at the time was very dirty and in a soft condition and the heavy vans would have cut the place up very badly. Having consulted the Clerk and Vice-Chairman, Mr. Day was allowed to stand in the Market Place, leaving over 18 feet roadway past the show.

Having had a number of other applications from showmen for shows on the HIRING DAY, he, the Surveyor, had been instructed by the Highways Committee to ascertain the views of the residents in Railway Street and Market Place. He called upon 41 tradesmen and publicans, and found that 37 were in favour of the shows being in the town, 1 against and 3 neutral. He would propose to place none in Railway Street to the Market Place side of the Beck Bridge. Between the Bridge and the railway gates there was a piece of ground clear of the roadway proper, about 925 square yards in extent, and he should send the "steam horses" up into the extreme corner near the Railway side.

November, 1896

COMPLAINT FROM BUGTHORPE

Councillor Parker, said that he had received a complaint from Bugthorpe about an open sewer which ran right through the village and close past the school. A certain amount of the sewage ran into the drain from some cottages near at hand. He thought that it ought to be closed up. Councillor Elgey said that it was a dangerous sort of thing to close a sewer without a proper system of drainage. The Chairman said quite right and the matter was adjourned to the next meeting.

December, 1896

POCKLINGTON SEWERAGE SCHEME

After long months of patient waiting, the Pocklington Sewerage Scheme, as approved by the Local Government Board, is now in active progress. This was started on Tuesday with a gang of some 20 men, and already some 150 yards of 15in pipes have been layed from the filter beds towards Pocklington. Next week it is proposed to put in the effluent pipes from the filter beds to the Canal Head, afterwhich they will proceed with the laying of pipes to the town when some 60 men will be employed.

January, 1897

DISTRICT RATE

The Pocklington District general rate of 2s 8d in the pound realised £786 4s 8d, was then presented, approved and duly signed.

March, 1897

HULL – A CITY

To celebrate the raising of Hull to the rank of a City, the Mayor has arranged a luncheon at the Town Hall on the afternoon of the 5th August, 1897.

July, 1897

THE CITY CHARTER – HULL

Hull received the first Charter from a King nearly 600 years ago. Hull refused admission to a King 300 years ago. Hull has been made a City by a Queen.

July, 1897

FIRST CITY COUNCIL MEETING – HULL
– RISING YOUNG CITY,

Today's Council meeting was the first such meeting by the Council for the City of Kingston upon Hull. The Mayor, Councillor Morrill, at the opening of the proceedings said, that, since the last meeting, high honour had been conferred upon this ancient borough . It had pleased the Queen to elevate the town to the rank of a city. He was sure there was not an inhabitant of Hull who did not feel in some way gratified by the great mark of Royal favour.

They had amongst them some of the most eminent merchants and shipowners of any town in the Kingdom, and it was to the future of this rising young City might be even more glorious than the past, and that it might progress with even greater strides.

July, 1897